Answering the Questions of Collaborative Leadership

TERRI L. MARTIN CAMERON L. RAINS

Foreword by ROBERT J. MARZANO

Solution Tree | Press

555 North Morton Street
Bloomington, IN 47404
800.733.6786 (toll free) / 812.336.7700
FAX: 812.336.7790

email: info@SolutionTree.com
SolutionTree.com

Visit **go.SolutionTree.com/leadership** to download the free reproducibles in this book.

Printed in the United States of America

22 21 20 19 18 1 2 3 4 5

Library of Congress Cataloging-in-Publication Data

Names: Martin, Terri L., author. | Rains, Cameron L., author.
Title: Stronger together : answering the questions of collaborative leadership / Terri L. Martin and Cameron L. Rains.
Description: Bloomington : Solution Tree Press, [2018] | Includes bibliographical references and index.
Identifiers: LCCN 2017046577 | ISBN 9781945349263 (perfect bound)
Subjects: LCSH: Educational leadership.
Classification: LCC LB2806 .M368 2018 | DDC 371.2/011--dc23 LC record available at https://lccn.loc.gov/2017046577

Solution Tree
Jeffrey C. Jones, CEO
Edmund M. Ackerman, President

Solution Tree Press
President and Publisher: Douglas M. Rife
Editorial Director: Sarah Payne-Mills
Art Director: Rian Anderson
Managing Production Editor: Kendra Slayton
Senior Production Editor: Tonya Maddox Cupp
Senior Editor: Amy Rubenstein
Proofreader: Elisabeth Abrams
Text and Cover Designer: Abigail Bowen

To Stephen, who has provided continuous support to me on my leadership journey for over thirty years.

—Terri L. Martin

To Juli, whose encouragement and honesty help me become a better leader.

—Cameron L. Rains

ACKNOWLEDGMENTS

There are three people who influenced this book. Each of them has helped us grow as leaders in very different ways.

Richard DuFour—The ultimate teacher and leader, whose collaborative soul helped so many others grow and become more than they ever thought they could be. If the worth of a man is valued by the number of people he impacts, then Rick DuFour has eternal worth.

Robert J. Marzano—An educator's researcher who can make sense of what needs to be done in order to make the difference in the lives of all children. Not only does he know what works, but he also puts the information in a format that is usable and doable.

Jeff Jones—A businessman who built his business on being the support mechanism that enables others to be all they can be. His mission, which is always at the forefront and drives his work, is centered on advancing the work of others.

It is the support, encouragement, and lessons learned from these three people that made this book possible and changed our lives forever.

Solution Tree Press would like to thank the following reviewers:

Robyn Elswood
Principal
Sunrise Elementary School
Shelley, Idaho

Amy Haynes
Principal
Columbus Middle School
Columbus, Nebraska

Kelly McCloughan
Principal
Arnold Elementary School
Michigan Center, Michigan

Paul Nolan
Principal
Redmond High School
Redmond, Oregon

Nicki Pack
Principal
Fairview Elementary School
Idaho Falls, Idaho

Leslie Roach
Principal
Northwood High School
Irvine, California

Visit **go.SolutionTree.com/leadership** to download the free reproducibles in this book.

TABLE OF CONTENTS

Reproducibles are in italics.

CHAPTER FIVE

CHAPTER SIX

EPILOGUE

ABOUT THE AUTHORS

Terri L. Martin is executive vice president of business development at Solution Tree and Marzano Research. Terri recently served as the director of the Regional Educational Laboratory for the central region, where she supported the creation of resources and deliverables to meet regional needs. Previously, she was the director of school improvement initiatives at the Missouri Department of Elementary and Secondary Education, where she led large projects to develop training programs and create professional learning communities statewide. She has developed and taught several courses as an adjunct professor at the University of Missouri and Columbia College while also serving as an elementary teacher and principal for almost twenty years.

Terri has provided professional development in over thirty states and several Canadian and Australian provinces. She has presented at Solution Tree, Association for Supervision and Curriculum Development, National Association of Elementary School Principals, and National Staff Development Council (currently Learning Forward) conferences. Terri is the author of *Improving Student Achievement: An Educational Leader's Guide for Developing Purposeful Schools* and a chapter in *The Collaborative Administrator: Working Together as a Professional Learning Community*.

She earned a bachelor of science degree from Stephens College. She earned master of education degrees in early childhood education and middle school administration, a specialist degree in elementary administration, and a doctorate in education in general administration from the University of Missouri.

To learn more about Terri's work, follow @drtlm on Twitter.

Cameron L. Rains is the assistant superintendent of curriculum and instruction for Clark-Pleasant Community School Corporation. In this role, he is part of a team working to ensure that all students in the district learn at high levels. Cameron also serves as a Marzano Research associate, where he delivers professional development on a wide range of topics across the United States. Previously, Cameron served as a teacher and instructional coach, and he acquired almost ten years of administrative experience as a director of elementary education and director of curriculum and instruction.

Cameron is passionate about school and district leadership and applying research findings in the school environment. He coauthored an article on the importance of reading fluency for *Reading and Writing Quarterly* and is coauthor of the book *Leading a High Reliability School.*

Cameron earned a bachelor of science degree in elementary education and a master of science degree in educational leadership from Indiana University. He also holds an educational specialist degree and a doctorate in educational leadership from Ball State University.

To learn more about Cameron's work, follow @CameronRains on Twitter.

To book Terri L. Martin or Cameron L. Rains for professional development, contact pd@SolutionTree.com.

FOREWORD

By Robert J. Marzano

Stronger Together by Terri L. Martin and Cameron L. Rains is both straightforward and unique in its approach to leadership. It is straightforward in the sense that it makes the case that no one can lead effectively in isolation. Just as it takes a village to educate a child, it takes a team to lead the school that educates that child. Interestingly, this relates directly to the burgeoning field of collective efficacy. At its most basic level and as it relates to K–12 schooling, collective efficacy means that teachers and leaders in a building truly believe that they can have more of a positive impact on students if they work as an integrated team, than they can if they operate as individuals.

While this simple premise has been articulated before, albeit expressed in different ways, it has previously not been articulated in steps as concrete as those that Martin and Rains provide. They propose six questions that, when answered, allow leaders to marshal the collaborative efforts of educators in a building or district in such a way that collective efficacy is a natural byproduct.

Question 1: What kind of leader am I? There is no correct answer to this question. However, its answer should provide a leader with clear guidance on how to interact with others. Specifically, leaders should emphasize and capitalize on their own strengths.

Question 2: How can I earn trust? The answer to this question is less open ended than is the answer to the first question. More specifically, Martin and Rains demonstrate that trust is earned by demonstrating intensity, empathy, accessibility, and humility.

Question 3: How do I build teams? The answer to this question should be guided by the growing body of work on the PLC process. Specifically, leaders should assemble different teams to meet the specific needs of their schools. When doing so, they should utilize the expertise of others and ensure stakeholder representation.

Question 4: How can I help develop a vision? This question involves specific actions a leader should take. Martin and Rains recommend that leaders begin by differentiating facts from beliefs since it is beliefs that are the basis for visions. But visions must be realistic, and facts can serve to help hone visions into an attainable yet inspiring possible future. Obviously, a school's vision should be shared by all relevant stakeholders and used by the leader to generate commitment to concrete goals that are grounded in the vision.

Question 5: How can I support teams? As before, the answer to this question should be guided by established PLC practices. These include examining common times; creating team tools; focusing on curriculum, instruction, and assessment; examining data; and monitoring progress.

Question 6: What, when, and how should I communicate? Arguably, this last question is the most important since it deals with day-to-day interactions with others. The quality of these interactions most probably has a one-to-one relationship with the quality of one's leadership. High-quality interactions involve listening to others, sharing with others, and celebrating others.

Stronger Together not only affirms a belief held by many leaders but also provides actionable guidance for actualizing this belief.

INTRODUCTION
Beginning Thoughts

No one can lead alone. After all, an educational leader's day can easily include a student missing the bus, an accident occurring in the pick-up lane, a teacher calling in sick, the cafeteria running out of cereal, and a bathroom pipe leaking—all in the first thirty minutes of the day and having nothing to do with learning. The responsibilities are too much for a single individual, with expectations of proficiency not only in management but also in pedagogy, instruction, assessment, curriculum, technology, research, staff evaluation processes, data analysis, and more. When you add making sure teachers have what they need and ensuring that students show academic growth, you can easily see that leadership is not a one-person job. It requires collaboration. But there is a way to protect sanity, strengthen organizations, and increase success: leading collaboratively.

Collaborative leadership requires someone to recognize and utilize the strengths of many people toward a single goal or vision. A collaborative leader fosters leadership skills in others and empowers them to be responsive to an organization's needs. It is not enough to understand the required work and accomplish the goals that are tied to that work. After all, great leaders do not lead tasks; great leaders lead people. Working in tandem with and promoting leadership in colleagues not only supports an organization but also facilitates goal achievement. Richard DuFour (2015) offers this blunt but true message: "No one person has the energy, expertise, and influence to fulfill all the responsibilities of your job successfully. If you try to do it all by yourself, you will fail" (p. 225). To wit, author Linda Lambert (1998) states that "when we equate the powerful concept of leadership with the behaviors of one person, we are limiting the achievement of broad-based participation by a community or a society" (p. 5). A broader leadership community makes the difference.

The following sections in this introduction define collaborative leadership, this book's audience and framework, and our hopes for you, the reader.

EXAMINING YOUR CURRENT REALITY

As you read this chapter, consider the following questions. Reflect on your personal growth as a leader and your support of growing leadership within your organization.

- How do you feel at the end of the day?
- What does your to-do list look like?
- Who supports you, and how do they provide that support?
- In what ways does that support improve your school's educational environment?
- How do you support those around you?
- How does that support grow others' leadership skills?

Visit ***go.SolutionTree.com/leadership*** *for a free reproducible version of this feature box.*

Collaborative Leadership

Collaborative leadership is about capitalizing on the strengths and skills of others in the effort to achieve common goals. It is understanding that success is achieved through sharing leadership responsibility. While *collaboration* is people working together, *collaborative leadership* is about encouraging others to be leaders as well.

Collaborative leadership incorporates various approaches and tools. These types of leaders strive to know themselves as leaders and endeavor to know others within the organization, establishing rapport that eventually leads to trust. Trust is crucial to collaboration, since "psychological safety, more than anything else, [is] critical to making a team work" (Duhigg, 2016). Collaborative leaders intentionally bring out others' strengths and potentials and use visioning to allow for greater autonomy. Tim Kanold (2011) encourages leaders to "paint that picture and let everyone touch the brush" (p. 31). Communication is a way to connect the people and the work. Author and motivational speaker Marcus Buckingham (2005) speaks to the necessity of leaders communicating clearly to connect an organization's purpose with the actions of those who live within to ensure progress.

Leaders use their knowledge of others to identify who should lead teams. After doing so, they relinquish authority to a broader group but continue providing support, thus enabling additional leaders to grow. They help their teams stay focused and working toward their shared vision. Director of qualitative research for the

Education Leadership Research Center at Texas A&M University, Jean Madsen (1996), says it precisely:

> In these communal settings, leadership is not defined as exercising power over others but as empowering people to accomplish shared goals. The open exercise of wit and will, principle and passion, time and talent, and purpose and power allow these varied participants to accomplish a set of goals. (p. 79)

This collaborative leadership allows everyone to use his or her personal strengths. Leadership authors Jim Kouzes and Barry Posner (2012) talk about this as creating a climate that promotes people being at their best. The two go on to share that, "in a climate of competence and confidence, people don't hesitate to hold themselves personally accountable for results, and they feel profound ownership for their achievements" (p. 243). People feel empowered to do what needs to be done when leaders enable this approach. Communities author Peter Block's (2013) words hold true: "Empowerment embodies the belief that the answer to the latest crisis lies within each of us" (p. 19).

Effective leaders first provide direction and then shift their energy to serve those who can get the job done. After providing direction, these leaders identify and meet the needs of the team with resources and tools (Hunter, 2004) and the needs of its individual members (acknowledging that people have their own fears, joys, and sensitivities). Richard DuFour, Rebecca DuFour, Robert Eaker, Thomas Many, and Mike Mattos (2016) refer to this group as a *guiding coalition*. They are a conduit for all other teams. Many schools simply call this a *leadership team*. What you call the teams is not as important as ensuring alignment between the leader and the teams' actions.

This Book's Audience

This book is written by educators, for educators. With almost fifty years of combined education experience in over thirty states (including our own settings), we have worked with many leaders from multiple levels. We have seen many leadership styles. We have seen leaders move from shaky ground to solid. One consistency is that when you know how to promote leadership in others, you accomplish amazing things. Anyone in an educational leadership position, from teacher leaders to those at the central office level, or anyone who desires such a position, can use this book to learn about and develop skills such as earning trust, visioning, and communicating, which are crucial to collaborative leadership.

Whether you aspire to leadership or have already spent years in a leadership position, this book can help. For those new to leadership, the reflection questions can hone your thoughts and strengthen your approaches. Experienced leaders know that finding new ideas and tools is worthwhile. Like a good collaborative leader, this book works with you and provides the information and resources you need to promote positive organizational growth.

This Book's Framework

Each chapter title is a common collaborative leadership question, and the chapter contents explore each question in turn. In our look at collaborative leadership, we began with an internal approach—look at yourself as a leader first. Chapter 1 asks you to think about your leadership skills, and the action steps help you increase those skills. Building trust from others is one of the most necessary skills. Chapter 2 reveals the need for building trust when leading others collaboratively and offers steps for doing just that. After you build trust, it is time to build a team of leaders. Chapter 3 helps you build efficacious teams of other collaborative leaders. Ensuring that everyone on the team is on the same page and using that to promote growth occur when they develop a common vision. Chapter 4 helps you create a vision in a way that promotes shared beliefs. The vision not only provides direction but also helps define the work you need to accomplish. Chapter 5 helps you guide the work that occurs in a collaboratively led educational environment. It is easy to get immersed in the work and stop seeing the bigger picture. Chapter 6 focuses on what, when, and how to communicate regarding the work and the resulting success. The book's epilogue brings home what we hope you've learned as you read.

Each chapter explores an aspect stemming from our work with administrators, superintendents, and teacher leaders in a variety of K–12 educational settings. The goal is to provide deeper understanding, strategies, and tools to support leaders who are working to grow other leaders. In hopes that you can examine your daily practices and compare them with what you learn as you read the book, we begin every chapter with several questions, prompting you to examine your current reality around leadership.

To help you think about possible changes, we conclude each chapter with action steps and reproducibles. Visit **go.SolutionTree.com/leadership** to access the free reproducibles in this book. We offer additional action steps there for creating and attaining goals and leading the right work. Because one of the best ways to move forward is to recognize individual staff members' and the whole school's accomplishments and progress, we also include a celebration idea or strategy in each chapter. You can implement these steps and tools as-is, or adjust them to fit your current reality.

In each chapter, we propose the following questions.

- What are you doing right now that fits with what you learned from reading this chapter?
- What might you stop doing after reading this chapter?
- What might you start doing after reading this chapter?

Reflect on the questions in light of each chapter's topic.

Our Hopes for You

Rather than stalling out on theory, we want to push your collaborative leadership efforts forward. We want to move your leadership thinking from isolation to collaboration, with the goals of increasing your collaborative leadership efficacy so that student achievement increases. You want results that show student growth. If the end result is to improve and increase student learning, then your challenge is to figure out how to encourage and support those who are responsible for getting it done. This book helps you meet that challenge by guiding you on the aspects of leading collaboratively and providing tools that help you grow as a leader.

We hope that regardless of where you currently are, reading this book will help you increase your understanding. You can connect what you learn from the book with the way you practice leadership. Chances are you already have some sort of leadership team in place. Do you know and understand members' strengths? Are you using them to reach team goals? If not, challenge yourself to expand your leadership abilities. What should you do first? Have you built the necessary trust? Do you have a common vision? You can choose new ways to look at leadership and new skills to practice. Finally, you can watch the impact your learning has on others. Is greater growth occurring? (We have included many reproducibles you can use to see various aspects of growth.) If so, you are a collaborative leader who is creating a successful learning environment that will profoundly benefit the staff, the community, and most important, the students.

CHAPTER ONE

What Kind of Leader Am I?

Are some people just born with the necessary charisma and drive to lead? Or do people learn the necessary skills along the way? Whether you believe leadership is innate or learned, self-knowledge is critical to its efficacy, a fact that debunks the myth that some people have just the right combination of characteristics to lead others. Harvard Business School professor Bill George (2011) says his research bears this out and that the "essence of leadership comes from not having predefined characteristics. Rather, it comes from knowing yourself—your strengths and weaknesses." Collaborative leaders are at their best when they know who they are and what they can do.

Prolific leadership writer Jack Canfield (2005) confirms that "you have to believe in yourself. Whether you call it self-esteem, self-confidence, or self-assurance, it is a deep-seated belief that you have what it takes—the abilities, inner resources, talents, and skills to create your desired results" (p. 40). A collaborative leader has a strong sense of self. Think about this as you reflect on the current reality surrounding who you are as a leader.

In this chapter, we talk about the skills necessary for you to become a collaborative leader, including truly knowing yourself as one. We ask you to assess your trustworthiness, visioning abilities, and communication styles. Finally, we discuss how you can recognize and enhance your strengths. The end of the chapter includes action steps for increasing your leadership skills. Because improving general leadership skills is the goal here, the steps in this chapter assume you're working with an assembled team. We explain how to assemble teams in chapter 3 (page 27).

EXAMINING YOUR CURRENT REALITY

As you read this chapter, consider the following questions. Reflect on your personal growth as a leader and your support of growing leadership within your organization.

- What skills do you bring to the leadership position?
- Why are these skills important?
- What difference do they make?
- What are your challenge areas?
- What difficulties do they cause?
- How do you compensate for them?

Visit ***go.SolutionTree.com/leadership*** *for a free reproducible version of this feature box.*

Understand Yourself as a Leader

There is a difference between knowing yourself and knowing what kind of leader you are. You may have many great attributes, such as a strong memory or a positive persona. It is good to be aware of those, but how do they affect you as a leader? This understanding is partly about relating what you know to how you would (or would not) use it to support and move an organization forward. It is also thinking about how you think and act in given situations. Self-assessment includes not only metacognition (thinking about your thinking) but also comparing yourself to others in social situations (Gilbert, Giesler, & Morris, 1995). It is a good idea to seek feedback from honest, trusted friends and family as well as anonymous feedback from colleagues. Your perception may be different from that of others.

After taking stock from colleagues, friends, and family, consider looking into a more objective approach. One way to do this is via a data-based personal inventory test such as the Leadership Practices Inventory, or LPI (Kouzes & Posner, 2012; www.leadershipchallenge.com). This inventory, based on years of research, focuses on five distinct practices: Model the Way, Inspire a Shared Vision, Challenge the Process, Enable Others to Act, and Encourage the Heart. Different inventories have different areas of emphasis.

Data-based inventories focus on specific characteristics crucial to effective leadership. For instance, professors Murray Barrick and Michael Mount (1991) tested five personality characteristics (www.outofservice.com/bigfive) and scored how relevant each was in different occupational groups. Their results show that conscientiousness is consistently important. Extraversion predicts managerial and training proficiency, and openness to new experiences correctly predicts how proficient someone is at training others (Barrick & Mount, 1991). Assess your conscientiousness and extraversion. Are you detail oriented about work and careful with others' feelings? Do you easily begin conversations with others, even with people you don't know? Professor and leadership author Linda Lambert (1998) asserts that the required skills include helping a team "develop a shared sense of purpose with colleagues, facilitate group processes, communicate well, understand transitions and change and their effects on people, mediate conflict, and hold a keen understanding of adult learning from a constructivist perspective" (p. 18). A *constructivist* perspective supports learning from experience. Leaders construct their own knowledge from their experiences and reflect on the results of those experiences.

What if, after assessing yourself for those qualities, whether through an official personality inventory, gathered feedback, or private self-reflection, you discover that you are not naturally extraverted or particularly conscientious? You can work to develop those skills in yourself, just as you can help others work on it; at the end of this chapter, you will find action steps for improving your leadership skills. Research shows that improving your skills also increases your metacognitive abilities, which will help you assess others' strengths, thereby aiding collaboration (Kruger & Dunning, 1999). You can read a book, attend a workshop, or take a class. You can make a concerted effort.

You mustn't have every strength to effectively lead. The collaborative aspect of tapping into others' strengths helps bolster change because you can build teams of people who have the strengths you lack. For example, you might excel at focusing people on getting things done, but be inexperienced at supporting the people who do the work. See who around you has this particular skill.

Focus on Trustworthiness, Visioning Ability, and Communication Style

Self-awareness helps build authenticity and trust; avoiding repeat mistakes is a side benefit of this knowledge. Author Kevin Cashman (2014) asserts that "when we are self-aware, we are more in touch with reality; people trust and respect us more." Completing the "My Leadership Challenges" worksheet (page 14) will help you pinpoint areas that need strengthening. Trustworthiness, visioning ability, and communication style—all important aspects of leading well—are touched on in the following sections and discussed at length in later chapters. In addition to the following strategies, there are action steps for improving your leadership skills at the end of this chapter (page 12).

Trustworthiness

Kouzes and Posner (2012) assert that trust is collaborative teamwork's "lifeblood," and that it is crucial to maintaining lasting relationships (p. 239). Collaborative leaders show their trustworthiness in everything they do—delivering on promises, doing what they say they are going to do, and living by example. If they break trust (or even just appear to), they work with individuals to discover what happened and figure out how to build back that trust again. For an in-depth look at earning trust, see chapter 2 (page 17).

Visioning Ability

Visioning ability means how well you work with others to create and sustain a vision. This ability is paramount to collaborative leadership success. Tim Kanold (2011) explains that the resulting "vision answers the question, Are we really doing what matters?" (p. 12). Collaborative leaders use the vision as a guide for all they do and lead a school to that vision. Chapter 4 (page 41) defines vision and addresses committing to one.

Communication Style

Open, honest dialogue is one of the best ways to communicate. It is also helpful to be sure everyone has the same understanding of the language because words have different meanings, implications, and connotations (DuFour et al., 2016). Collaborative leaders use good communication to help them help others move forward. Chapter 6 (page 67) details communication strategies for different audiences.

While keeping conversations positive is important, you cannot avoid difficult conversations. Dennis Sparks (2010), in his book on daily meditations for school leaders, says, "Intentionally increasing the number of positive interactions with members of the school community can transform relationships and improve school culture" (p. 39). We strongly believe that positive interactions will hold you in good stead when you have more difficult ones.

Promote Your Strengths

Leaders who understand their own strengths, perhaps through an assessment such as this chapter's "My Leadership Strengths" worksheet (page 13) or the LPI (Kouzes & Posner, 2012), can use those strengths to build trust, create vision and buy-in, communicate effectively, and help create growth. For example, leaders who are visionary can use that skill to paint a picture of the future and guide others in that direction. Similarly, detail-oriented leaders might gather others together to create a detailed plan that shows the steps necessary to move toward a designated end line. Leaders can make most strengths work.

Let others know who you are. If you can jump right into a task and complete it, make that fact apparent. Share your strengths with others, and let them know that you are available to assist them whenever anyone needs those strengths.

A benefit of collaborative leadership is that no one person has to have all the necessary skills or strengths for any given situation; a good collaborative leader capitalizes on strengths from others. For example, a collaborative leader who needs to give detailed instructions to others but lacks that particular strength knows who could get the job done right; that leader delegates the task appropriately.

Note that a leader's understanding of his or her personal weaknesses is not synonymous with being a weak leader. This realization might actually be one of the biggest lessons you can learn from your self-assessment. There is often a perception that a leader cannot have any weaknesses. Everyone has weaknesses. How you handle them makes the difference.

In the end, personal understanding of a leader's strengths and weaknesses enables growth. See "My Leadership Strengths" (page 13) and "My Leadership Challenges" (page 14) at the end of this chapter to jumpstart that understanding. They promote reflection on each of these in order to grow as a leader. Finally, "Celebrating My Strengths" (page 15) helps you focus on positives. Leaders need to take time to recognize themselves and acknowledge when they have used their strengths to move an organization forward. Seeking honest feedback about your strengths and weaknesses is important, too. George (2011) encourages getting that feedback from other leaders and your superiors, as well as from those you lead.

Conclusion

In this chapter, we answered the question, What kind of leader am I? Take time answering the following questions, and think critically about each.

- What are you doing right now that fits with what you learned from reading this chapter?
- What might you stop doing after reading this chapter?
- What might you start doing after reading this chapter?

Action Steps for Improving Your Leadership Skills

Think about your current leadership abilities, whether you are currently leading a team of people or not. Consider the following two steps.

1. Identify your own leadership strengths.
    - Using the "My Leadership Strengths" worksheet (page 13), list between three and five of your personal leadership strengths.
    - Brainstorm ways you can use these strengths.
    - Record when you use these strengths and the impact they have had.
2. Identify your own leadership challenges.
    - Using the "My Leadership Challenges" worksheet (page 14), list between three and five of your personal leadership challenges.
    - Brainstorm ways you can strengthen those areas.

My Leadership Strengths

List at least three of your personal leadership strengths. Then brainstorm possible results of using those strengths.

Strength: What is it, and how do I use it?	
Trait	Result

Strength: What is it, and how do I use it?	
Trait	Result

Strength: What is it, and how do I use it?	
Trait	Result

My Leadership Challenges

List at least three of your personal leadership challenges. Then brainstorm ways you can strengthen those areas.

Challenge: What is it, and how can I strengthen this area?	
Trait	Strengthening Ideas

Challenge: What is it, and how can I strengthen this area?	
Trait	Strengthening Ideas

Challenge: What is it, and how can I strengthen this area?	
Trait	Strengthening Ideas

Celebrating My Strengths

List at least three of your personal leadership strengths. Keep a running log of when you used them and why.

Strength: What is it, and when did I use it in a positive way?	
Trait	Use

Strength: What is it, and when did I use it in a positive way?	
Trait	Use

Strength: What is it, and when did I use it in a positive way?	
Trait	Use

CHAPTER TWO

How Can I Earn Trust?

In collaborative leadership, trust is essential. Research bears this out. Educational professors Megan Tschannen-Moran and Wayne K. Hoy's (1998) study demonstrates a significant direct correlation between trust and how often a teacher collaborates with the principal and with colleagues: "Faculty trust is an important aspect of the openness and health of school climate. It is related to the authenticity of both the principal's and the teachers' behavior" (p. xx). You will find action steps for building trust later in this chapter (page 22).

While trust is critical, its existence is not always obvious. Joel Peterson (2016) discusses how when trust is low, organizations move toward using power as an influencer—that doesn't coincide with collaboration. On the other hand, when one person trusts another, he or she spends less energy protecting him- or herself and, therefore, feels safe to take risks (Edmonson, 2004; Jarvenpaa, Knoll, & Leidner, 1998). That feeling is known as *psychological safety* (Edmonson, 2004).

Anthony S. Bryk, president of the Carnegie Foundation for the Advancement of Teaching, and Barbara Schneider (2002), Michigan State University College of Education distinguished professor, say you can get an idea of how well teachers trust their principal by how they address the statements on page 18 about trustworthy characteristics. Depending on the leadership structure and the setting, these statements could be adapted to say team leader, leadership team, superintendent, or other leaders. Visit **go.SolutionTree.com/leadership** for a link to these statements.

Consider asking your teams to anonymously address these statements at the end of each semester to get a clear idea of where you stand.

- It's OK in this school to discuss feelings, worries, and frustrations with the principal.
- The principal looks out for the personal welfare of the faculty members in this school.
- I take the principal at his or her word.
- The principal in this school is an effective manager, who makes the school run smoothly.
- The principal places students' needs ahead of his or her political interests.
- The principal has confidence in the teachers' expertise.
- The principal is personally interested in teachers' professional development.
- I really respect my principal as an educator.
- I feel that the principal respects me. (Bryk & Schneider, 2002, p. 157)

When leaders ensure that colleagues can confirm these statements, the result is increased teacher collaboration and student achievement (Vodicka, 2006). Creating a culture that affirms these questions requires efforts on several interpersonal fronts. The following sections focus on those fronts, including demonstrating integrity, practicing empathy, making yourself accessible, and understanding the need for humility.

EXAMINING YOUR CURRENT REALITY

As you read this chapter, consider the following questions. Reflect on your personal growth as a leader and your support of growing leadership within your organization.

- How do you define trustworthiness?
- Name three people you trust and why you trust them.
- How do you gain trust from someone?
- How do you know that you have gained someone's trust?

*Visit **go.SolutionTree.com/leadership** for a free reproducible version of this feature box.*

Demonstrate Integrity

Collaborative leaders show integrity. This is a crucial element of trust (Whitener, Brodt, Korsgaard, & Werner, 1998), because "above all, people want to believe in their leaders. They want to believe that the leaders' word can be trusted, that they do what they say" (Kouzes & Posner, 1999, p. 131). Integrity manifests itself in many ways, including honesty, commitment, and consistency. For example, several studies demonstrate that "highly regarded principals demonstrate honesty and commitment to follow through—in all interactions with faculty, support staff, parents, and students" (Barlow, 2001; Blase & Blase, 2001; Sebring & Bryk, 2000, as cited in Brewster & Railsback, 2003). Consistency, one of Devin Vodicka's (2006) four elements of trust, piggybacks off commitment; trust is established when a person continually does what we expect of him or her. Consistency between what a leader says and what he or she does, from person to person and from day to day, points to integrity—congruence in talk and action. A mindful collaborative leader shows integrity even when a situation is more easily handled another way. Collaborative leaders let others see their belief systems via verbal responses to everyday actions.

Relationships are easier to build when the leader projects consistency. For example, if a leader's belief is that all students can learn, then that leader's actions would consistently illustrate that belief. Something as simple as having an informal conversation with a colleague during which you say that one student is not going to succeed in school can lead to a need to later justify that statement. That misalignment may cause team members to fear misalignment in other areas between your thoughts and your actions. From simple things, such as informal conversations, to complex issues, such as assessment practices, the leader projects consistency.

Practice Empathy

Beware of focusing so much on data and vision that you forget that people are at the heart of what is happening. When you take time to know another person—and let another person know you—and all that entails (revealing intimacies and vulnerabilities about yourself, for example), you gain trust. Being mindful of human needs—practicing empathy—isn't specific only to personal relationships:

> The behaviors that create psychological safety . . . are part of the same unwritten rules we often turn to, as individuals, when we need to establish a bond. And those human bonds matter as much at work as anywhere else. In fact, they sometimes matter more. (Duhigg, 2016)

This trust scaffolds the team's work. Collaborative leaders show empathy, an element of compassion (Vodicka, 2006), by getting to know team members and understanding who they are both personally and professionally (Sebring & Bryk, 2000). And this doesn't mean just discussing favorite sports teams or the latest film releases (see the "Connecting Our Thinking" questionnaire on page 25). Even data-driven team-building research encourages "emotional conversations and discussions of norms" (Duhigg, 2016). The self-disclosure required of empathy is a form of risk taking. Remember that to feel psychologically safe while taking risks is a matter of trust

(Edmonson, 2004). There are ways to move a person or team into nonthreatening conversations where they learn more about each other. Generic conversation starters can help move past casual conversation. For example, talking about a recent movie you saw may encourage others to pick up that thread. This is especially helpful if you avoid including personal qualifiers such as "It was great" or "It was awful."

Effective collaborative leaders intentionally add ways for others to get to know one another into the day's routine. This effort can be as simple as creating a bulletin board in the faculty lounge where people share about themselves, integrating activities into faculty or team meetings (such as "Find Someone Who" on page 23), or including information about individuals in a weekly newsletter (see the "All About You" newsletter example on page 24). They also make sure they are "available to teachers, parents, students, and staff" (Blase & Blase, 2001; Sebring & Bryk, 2000, as cited in Brewster & Railsback, 2003).

However, a trusting relationship does not have to be a friendship. It can simply be a way to interact with another person with professional respect and understanding. It provides a platform for two or more people to interact with one another. The leader's relationship with collaborative team members is the starting point for getting work done. For example, if you are unsure how to accomplish an assigned task but are confident in the relationship, you are more likely to begin the work because you know you have the other person's support and can reach out for assistance.

Be Accessible

Because collaborative leadership is all about people, it only makes sense that people need to see others in action to make this work. Kouzes and Posner (2012) confirm that one of the most significant ways leaders can show they care is by being available. Don't hide behind your desk. Accessibility and visibility are key. Show you care by being in the work and with people. Because more people are involved in the work, there is a greater need to be accessible. That way, issues, concerns, and celebrations are readily shared and addressed.

Understand the Need for Humility

Humility is a required part of trust building. A large part of effective collaborative leadership means giving up what might be perceived as power in order to share the leadership. Your challenge is to educate all others about this perspective, so that misperceptions don't prevent collaboration from flourishing. Dedicating time at a faculty meeting to defining collaborative leadership and its implications for the school is a great way to start. Depending on the school culture, it might be a good idea to set up some parameters such as this: when you have a question, first consider who is most closely connected to leading the related work. If it is a team leader, go to that person first for answers.

Sharing leadership is sometimes tough when a leader is struggling with a situation, due to either lack of skills or lack of knowledge. Some leaders think that if they don't have all the answers, they lack a necessary leadership skill. Tim Kanold (2011) states that "humility is acknowledging that no individual adult will ever have all the answers and that effective teaching and learning *require* the pursuit of continuous improvement and growth" (p. 91).

You can learn a great deal about leaders, and form significant perceptions of who they are, by watching how they handle mistakes. Collaborative leaders embrace the fact that mistakes will happen, and instead of trying to hide the mistake or pretend it didn't happen, they are transparent about it. They take ownership of the mistake and work to resolve any issues. By being transparent when handling situations, both positive and negative, a collaborative leader models and guides others.

Conclusion

In this chapter, we answered the question, How can I earn trust? Take time answering the following questions, and think critically about each.

- What are you doing right now that fits with what you learned from reading this chapter?
- What might you stop doing after reading this chapter?
- What might you start doing after reading this chapter?

Action Steps for Building Trust

Although sharing survey results can be difficult, especially when the results are negative, it is an important part of building trust. To maintain integrity, it is important to ensure that the sharing consists of openness, honesty, and lack of blame, with a focus on using the information to move forward in a positive direction. Consider the following four steps.

1. Include activities during regularly scheduled meetings so people who work together can get to know one another informally. Include yourself in the activities so that you show authenticity.
    - Ice breakers include a scavenger hunt called "Find Someone Who" (page 23).
2. Share team-building activities with leaders and have them report trust-building progress quarterly. It might be beneficial to have the leaders work with their teams to define how they will be reporting that trust is being built in the teams.
    - Use the "All About You" questionnaire (page 24) to collect information about members and, with consent, share the information in a newsletter or on a bulletin board. Promote this as a way to celebrate the uniqueness of each individual.
3. Ensure you understand what is important to those you lead. This is not so you can always acquiesce but so you can cultivate empathy. Use the "Connecting Our Thinking" worksheet (page 25) to connect what team members deem important to your school's goals.
    - Find ways to provide direction while showing that what matters to others is important. This can be as simple as acknowledging someone's thinking in a faculty meeting or a newsletter.
4. Continuously track how others are feeling about what is happening in your school.
    - Create a survey or find one online. Multiple surveys on both trust and, more specifically, team trust, are available online. Search for those entries.
    - Allow participants to complete the survey anonymously, so you get more accurate information.
    - Analyze the information, format the data, share them with team members, celebrate the positive, and address the negative. When doing this, compile the data so they are easy for others to follow; ensure the meaning is clear.

Find Someone Who

Give each team member a copy of this worksheet. Ask them to "Find someone who . . . " fits the description of each square (or fewer squares, depending on your allotted time). This scavenger hunt helps team members get to know each other informally.

Plays a musical instrument	Volunteers for an organization	Failed his or her first driving test	Has called someone the wrong name	Flies a plane
Eschews social media	Speaks a foreign language	Likes being outdoors	Has three or more children	Loves football
Enjoys writing	Likes sushi	Free	Has a dog	Has been out of the country
Hates football	Knows how to juggle	Likes reality TV shows	Is an avid reader	Can convincingly mimic an animal
Has grandchildren	Has a cat	Has been to a rock concert	Is vegan	Has had stitches or a cast

All About You

Create an All About You section in the faculty and staff newsletter. This section could feature an individual staff member or a group. Consider the following three steps.

1. Send a questionnaire to each faculty and staff member at the beginning of the school year.
2. Make sure the template includes between three and five questions or categories, such as the following.
   a. My special talent or skill is ________________________________.
   b. I was born in ________________________________ and have lived in ________________________________.
   c. I would like to be known for ________________________________.
3. Two weeks after school starts, collect the completed questionnaires, and include a few in each newsletter or one per week on a bulletin board.

Connecting Our Thinking

Divide members into groups of four to six. Distribute one worksheet to each group and ask them to complete it. During discussion, you can connect what team members deem important to your school's goals. Consider the following four steps.

1. What is most important to you as we increase student achievement? Write up to ten ideas.

    - ______________________________
    - ______________________________
    - ______________________________
    - ______________________________
    - ______________________________
    - ______________________________
    - ______________________________
    - ______________________________
    - ______________________________
    - ______________________________

2. After you've written ten ideas, transcribe them to a piece of chart paper.
3. Compare the agreed-on school goals to the ideas created by the teams.
4. Where there are gaps, brainstorm ways we can align our personal thinking with that of the school. In this way, we can use our personal beliefs to further our school goals and have honest conversations when the two do not align.

CHAPTER THREE

How Do I Build Teams?

Creating collaborative teams involves choosing people for teams and supporting those individuals and teams in ways that promote both growth in the individuals and growth in the school. As we explain in this chapter, you are building collaborative teams *not* to delegate and accomplish more work. Instead, you are considering different kinds of teams, pulling together the right people once you understand their strengths, and utilizing their expertise so they can accomplish common goals. You are ensuring that stakeholders are represented across the building or district. And ultimately, by establishing loose-tight leadership, you are flexibly guiding while adhering to non-negotiables while simultaneously promoting the success of those doing the work.

EXAMINING YOUR CURRENT REALITY

As you read this chapter, consider the following questions. Reflect on your personal growth as a leader and your support of growing leadership within your organization.

- What makes the strongest teacher or building leaders the way they are?
- How do you tap into their strengths?
- In what leadership positions do you place them?
- To meet targeted goals, what types of leadership do you need?
- How do you ensure that everyone feels represented in schoolwide decisions?
- What do you encourage and discourage?

Visit ***go.SolutionTree.com/leadership*** *for a free reproducible version of this feature box.*

Assemble Different Kinds of Teams

As a collaborative leader, you'll build different kinds of teams—teams that require different positions and serve different functions. Teams may be formed based on building, teacher, or student needs. Remember to organize teams based on needs and the resulting required tasks. Guiding coalitions provide leadership for the school as a whole. Guiding coalitions support collaborative teams, which typically ensure high levels of learning in each department or grade level, or support a specific school goal. The action steps later in this chapter (pages 34–35) help you build and support all kinds of teams.

Team Structures

Teams can have both a vertical and a horizontal structure. Vertically, they begin at the building level and end at the classroom level. For example, if a building is focusing on creating a safe and orderly climate, teams might be organized vertically with stakeholders who work in different capacities within the school (because safety and order are important across all classrooms, grade levels, departments, and the building as a whole). Conversely, if a school is focusing on creating a guaranteed and viable curriculum, teams might be organized horizontally with educators who teach the same course or grade level (so they can agree on the most important learning outcomes and then compare horizontally across a school or district).

Team Types

First, it is a good idea to build teams around the work that changes schools at large. They include building administrators and district administrators involved in improving student achievement (via curriculum, instruction, assessment, or special education) who communicate directly with each building staff, guiding coalition, and central office staff. This team typically discusses the goals and action plans established by each school's guiding coalition. They share what has worked well and solve issues that arise.

Second, begin assembling a *guiding coalition*. This team, which is common in educational settings, is specifically charged with leading change in a school. Leadership and change authority John Kotter (2012) states:

> Because major change is so difficult to accomplish, a powerful force is required to sustain the process. No one individual, even a monarch-like CEO, is ever able to develop the right vision, communicate it to large numbers of people, eliminate all the key obstacles, generate short-term wins, lead and manage dozens of change projects, and anchor new approaches deep in the organization's culture. Weak committees are even worse. A strong guiding coalition is always needed—one with the right composition, level of trust, and shared objective. (pp. 54–55)

The guiding coalition identifies necessary changes and develops implementation plans. Its members understand the change process, help move staff forward positively, and challenge the status quo when necessary. When assembling this team, choose teachers from multiple departments and grade levels, including department chairs, school improvement committee members, and parent, student, and teacher association representatives (Mattos, DuFour, DuFour, Eaker, & Many, 2016). Remember to "include opinion leaders—people who are so respected within the organization that others are likely to follow their lead" (Mattos et al., 2016, p. 21).

After assembling the guiding coalition, begin forming collaborative teams around a particular content area or grade level. For example, if a school seeks to increase students' writing abilities, a collaborative team might develop a writing continuum that describes where students are in their abilities; they would then ensure all staff understand the continuum, how to identify where students are on it, and how to instruct for increased writing achievement. This differs from grade-level or departmental collaborative teamwork because these teams typically address student learning outcomes specific to their course or grade level. Usually, a member from the guiding coalition leads a collaborative team so there is a defined connection both to leadership and among the teams themselves.

One of the most well-defined support systems is a Professional Learning Community at Work (PLC at Work™), as defined by educators DuFour et al. (2016), who explain it as a continuous process dedicated to helping students by working collaboratively "in recurring cycles of collective inquiry and action research" (p. 10) and ensuring that educators receive job-embedded learning. Though we encourage following a vetted process such as PLCs, it is not absolutely necessary for success. What is necessary are established structures and tools that support both the people and the work.

And keep your teams small. Harvard professor and team researcher J. Richard Hackman's (2002) research supports high engagement and performance from teams that have fewer than ten members. He warns that the "number of performance problems a team encounters increases *exponentially* as team size increases" (Hackman, 2002, as cited in Stark, 2002).

Regardless of how you decide to organize teams and who comprises them, be sure to communicate with all members about who their colleagues are. Research shows that being unclear about who is on a team is one of the three most common collaboration problems (Stark, 2002). In fact, according to one study, fewer than "10% of supposed team members agreed on who their teammates were. This finding raises the question: If teammates can't agree on whom they're collaborating with, how can they align on purpose and expectations?" (Rigoni & Nelson, 2016).

Understand and Utilize the Expertise of Others

A leader who understands others' strengths and weaknesses can create the most efficacious teams. For example, some people are naturally more in tune with others, whereas some people are more focused on tasks. It is usually easy to recognize when someone is more comfortable with people than the tasks, or vice versa. Relationship-oriented people thrive on working with and around others. They may enjoy bouncing ideas off or brainstorming with others. These people are usually good at ensuring that all voices are heard, and they can often provide ice breakers or team activities. In contrast, others might like getting into the details or striving toward completion. Providing these team members with to-do lists or letting them consider the action steps necessary to get to the big picture might be appropriate tasks. Still other people are more visionary and work best when they see the whole picture, moving toward a larger goal. They can contribute to team meetings by creating visual representations of an end goal or verbally articulating what it looks like. Collaborative leaders intentionally align each team member with work within his or her comfort areas.

Data culled from multiple studies over several years find four repeated leadership strength domains: (1) executing, (2) influencing, (3) relationship building, and (4) strategic thinking (Rath & Conchie, 2008). To understand more about each of the domains, look at table 3.1. You already assessed your own leadership skills and continued working on strengthening them, but the following information helps you assess others' strengths, which may not be apparent to you.

TABLE 3.1: Four Domains of Leadership Skills

Executing	Influencing	Relationship Building	Strategic Thinking
• Achieves • Arranges • Shows consistency • Shows conviction • Deliberates • Shows discipline • Focuses • Shows responsibility • Restores	• Activates • Commands • Communicates • Competes • Maximizes • Shows self-assuredness • Proves significant • Woos others	• Adapts • Develops • Connects • Empathizes • Includes others • Individualizes • Shows positivity • Relates	• Analyzes • Uses context • Envisions future • Idealizes • Offers input • Understands • Learns • Strategizes

Source: Adapted from Rath & Conchie, 2008.

One way to find out how people like to approach tasks is simply by asking. Use the "My Professional Strengths" worksheet (page 38) to help others articulate whether they are, for example, more focused, competitive, harmonious, or analytical. Ideally, ten or more people will complete the worksheet at a time, since they will discuss the results in groups afterward. Not only will this worksheet help individuals learn more about their own personal strengths, but it will help the group leader better understand how to structure the team. More often than not, people with like strengths are better able to communicate with one another. However, a team of individuals who each address a task the same way is not always the most productive. According to researchers, an ideal team has each of the four domains represented (Rath & Conchie, 2008). For example, if everyone is task oriented, who helps with understanding the big picture or keeps things moving? "Eighty Years of Accomplishments" (page 36) outlines clear professional goals and aspirations, which can determine team assignments, and the "From Mine to Ours" exercise (page 37) can you help and the other team members determine the team's strongest collective skills.

By assembling the right people, collaborative leaders do the same thing for them that they do for themselves: help them believe in their own leadership skills or potential, help them grow their personal strengths, and strengthen weaknesses. Forming guiding coalitions and collaborative teams based on various leadership styles and strengths increases the diversity of thought and, in turn, each team's potential.

Ensure Stakeholder Representation

While promoting and supporting leadership skills in others, the collaborative leader must also ensure that all stakeholders are represented. Not everyone will want to lead or have the skills your teams need, but everyone needs to have his or her voice heard. To be clear, while all voices should be heard, the imperative is ensuring that the outcome aligns with the vision. A guiding coalition goal is to help create in others an understanding and promote a willingness to work together to move forward (DuFour et al., 2016). This includes teachers, students, parents, and any outside organizations that significantly impact the school.

It is also a good idea to ensure a link to pertinent central office staff. Regardless of whether a team requires their input, their understanding and support are sometimes simply good to have. They can provide a different perspective—often from a larger, districtwide view. In addition, central office staff can often provide additional resources, including time, money, or expertise. Ensuring that people feel represented at the front end is well worth the time.

Establish Loose-Tight Leadership

It is important to have structure in a collaborative environment, to fend off the chaos that can so commonly occur in a school's day-to-day happenings, but it is equally important to provide autonomy. Collaborative leaders know and communicate both where there is flexibility (showing loose leadership) and elements that are non-negotiable (showing tight leadership). These two approaches, combined into loose-tight leadership, can promote success. Research supports this approach. According to a meta-analysis, schools with *defined autonomy* but strong commitment to common goals generate positive results for students (Marzano & Waters, 2009).

Non-negotiables are an integral part of team functioning, and they fall under several categories: (1) mandates, (2) mission or vision statement requirements, and (3) team structure. Have open, honest conversations about them. There will always be mandates, whether federal, state, or district specific. Those tied to student safety, for example, are likely to come from a district office. Educational entities with strong mission and vision statements will have additional non-negotiables, such as *all students are given the time they need to learn*; actions tied to that requirement are non-negotiable. And finally, some non-negotiables center on team structures. For example, many schools mandate that every staff member participate on a collaborative team. Or they might state exactly how often teams should meet. These non-negotiables almost always exist to assist with team governance. Most educators appreciate the non-negotiables as they provide both parameters and support.

Beyond non-negotiables, however, leaders are sharing power with others. Doing so builds leadership capacity and increases team members' ability to accomplish more. People who are beginning to understand collaborative leadership frequently ask how much power they should give up and how much they should keep. Harvard professor and team researcher J. Richard Hackman (2002, as cited in Stark, 2002) says:

> Leaders often err either by giving teams too much direction (for example, telling them not only what they are to accomplish but all the details about how they are to go about accomplishing it) or too little (for example, giving merely a vague description of the team's purposes and leaving it to the team to "work out the details"). Setting good direction for a team means being authoritative and insistent about desired end states, but being equally insistent about not specifying how the team should go about achieving those end-states.

DuFour et al.'s (2016) definition of loose-tight leadership in professional learning communities in their book *Learning by Doing*, can help new leaders decide what to let go of. DuFour et al. (2016) posit that loose leadership is when teachers have complete discretion; tight leadership is when decisions and actions are mandated. All staff are required to engage in tight work precisely the way it is outlined. This description, plus some trial and error, can help leaders determine what is loose and what is tight.

When deciding what to relinquish, consider what accountability looks like. Along with team members, define what each team is accountable for and what concrete evidence it will provide that it completed those tasks. Approach this by thinking about where the bottom line lies. When things go well, who will get credit? When they don't, who will take the blame? For example, increasing student achievement is everyone's responsibility, but when it comes right down to it, the classroom is where achievement occurs. As long as teachers are results oriented and hold themselves accountable for the results, they need the autonomy to make the decisions that get those results. Therefore, increased student achievement is non-negotiable, but how the teachers get students there is negotiable. Create a shared document with this information, review it at specified times, and highlight progress toward the goals. See chapter 5 (page 53) for more about establishing team norms, which applies to this process.

Conclusion

In this chapter, we answered the question, How do I build teams? Take time answering the following questions, and think critically about each.

- What are you doing right now that fits with what you learned from reading this chapter?
- What might you stop doing after reading this chapter?
- What might you start doing after reading this chapter?

Action Steps for Building and Supporting a Team

These seven action steps can aid your formation of a guiding coalition or collaborative teams (vertical or horizontal).

1. Observe the relationships among your building staff.
    a. Whom do people go to when they need support?
    b. Who exemplifies teaching and learning?
    c. Who is willing to always go the extra mile?
2. Think about ways to share your leadership.
    a. Explain to your staff your belief in shared leadership.
    b. Work with them to define what a leadership team should look like.
        i. Who needs to be represented?
        ii. How should information be shared?
        iii. What skills would a leadership team member need to possess?
        iv. How would a leadership team support everyone in the building?
3. Create a guiding coalition or collaborative team.
    a. Have your staff write recommendations for individuals for the leadership team. Each recommendation should include a justification.
    b. Gather these recommendations and review the strengths and weaknesses of each individual prior to deciding who needs to be on the team. Seek additional information as needed.
    c. Once the team is formed, build in exercises. For example, you can use the "Find Someone Who" scavenger hunt (page 23) to help members get to know each other better as individuals.
    d. Use the "Eighty Years of Accomplishments" worksheet (page 36) to gain a deeper understanding of the team members' professional and personal goals and aspirations. Use this information to look for commonalities regarding goals and aspirations to build continuity within the team. If commonalities are not present, discuss each person's goals to further understand his or her perspective.
4. Have your team complete the "My Professional Strengths" (page 38) and "My Leadership Challenges" worksheets (page 14) about their own leadership strengths and challenges.

page 1 of 2

5. On a large sheet of paper, draw a diagram like the one in the "From Mine to Ours" worksheet (page 37).
    a. Assign each team member a slice of the circle.
    b. Have each team member write the leadership skills he or she brings.
    c. After everyone has finished, have a group conversation during which the team compiles the skills most common for the group as a whole, and write those in the center circle.
6. Create a culture where everyone recognizes fellow team members. For example, at faculty meetings, have teachers share positive things that other teachers have done. Account for people who are sometimes left out, such as playground supervisors and bus drivers. Review these celebrations and recognitions to better understand the strengths and expertise that others demonstrate. Then enable those strengths within the team, recognizing when they are focused on positive change.
7. Define team actions.
    a. Make sure every group is represented.
    b. Make sure each team member is aware of what stakeholder he or she represents.
    c. Make sure team heads disseminate information, gather feedback, and support those in their defined group.
    d. Document every meeting with meeting minutes and have them readily available to all staff.
    e. Have all teams determine which member should complete the "Team Monitoring" worksheet (page 39). The worksheet ensures a protocol for bringing outside information to meetings and ensures that all members share the same information. Team members share the questions generated during their next team meeting. They capture and share the responses with the leadership team as a whole.

Eighty Years of Accomplishments

Ask each team member to complete this worksheet so you can gain a deeper understanding of the team members' professional and personal goals and aspirations. It, along with each person's strengths and weaknesses, will help you determine team placement.

Imagine your professional life after eighty years of commitment. Please list your top-three accomplishments from those years, and explain what they mean to you.

1.

2.

3.

From Mine to Ours

Assign each team member a slice of the circle, and have him or her write his or her leadership skills. This exercise can help you and other team members determine the team's strongest collective skills.

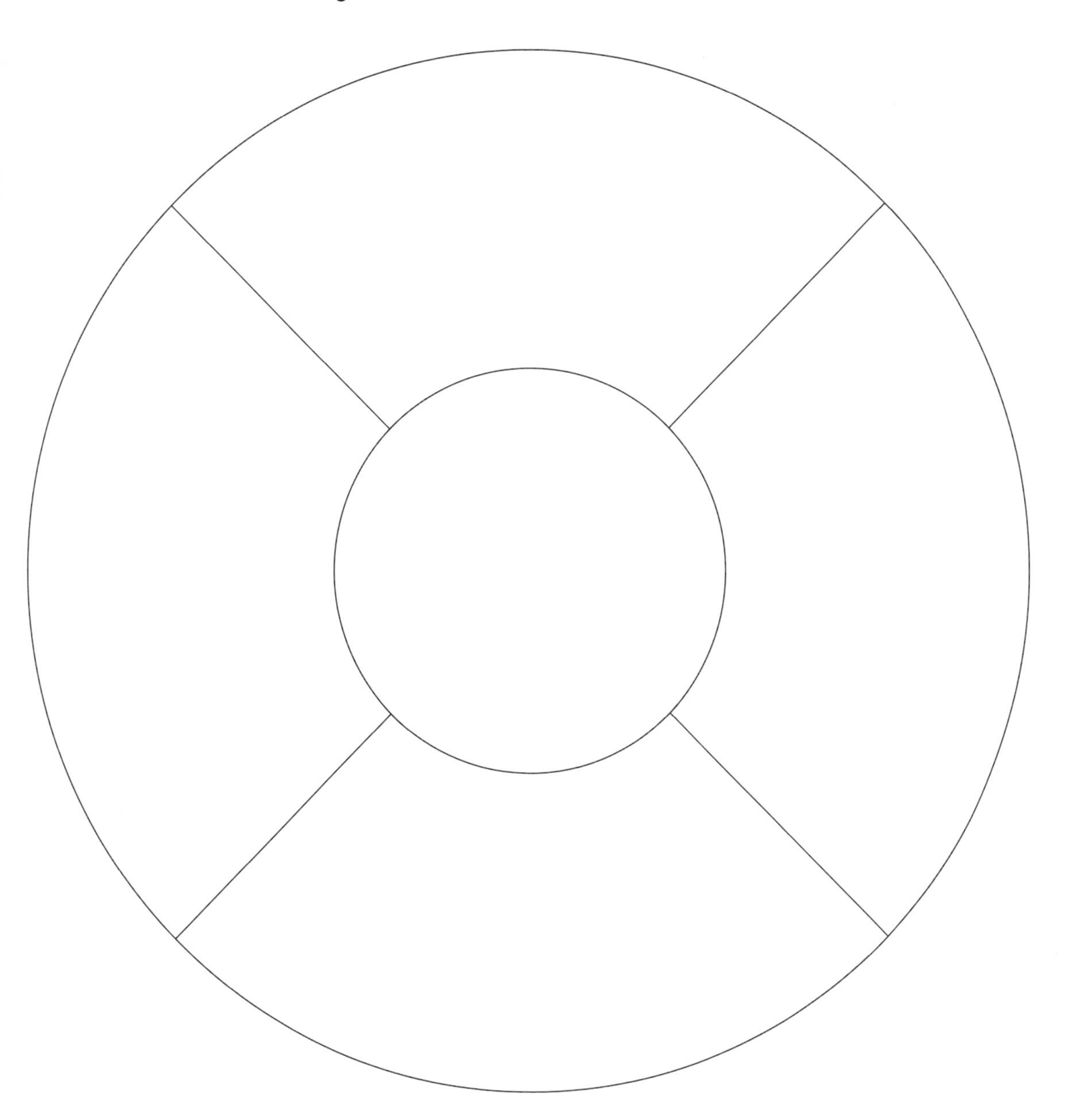

My Professional Strengths

People approach their professional journey in a variety of ways. It takes different types of people grouped together to attain goals. Each of the following statements illustrates an individual's strength.

For the purpose of this exercise, have each person decide which one of the four statements best applies. He or she might like all the statements, but should choose the one that most resonates.

- *I like knowing where we will end up.*
- *I like maximizing our resources.*
- *I like knowing who is going with me.*
- *I like figuring out how we are going to get there.*

Have people group themselves by the statement they chose. Within the groups, have people answer the following four questions.

1. Why is this statement important to us? List three reasons.
2. How does this statement increase our productivity? List three reasons.
3. How does this statement impact the other statements? List at least one way.
4. What would be our second choice? List at least one alternative.

After everyone has answered the questions, each group shares one or two answers with everyone. Then, have groups discuss again why it is important to understand that people made different choices.

Team Monitoring

Help teams stay focused on the agreed-on vision and goals by monitoring progress via routine check-ins and regular meetings.

Team (name and type): ____________________

Team leader: ____________________

Meeting date: ____________________

Major points to share from meeting:

1.

2.

3.

Questions to ask of team prior to the next meeting:

Responses from these questions:

CHAPTER FOUR

How Can I Help Develop a Vision?

It is difficult to find a school without some sort of vision statement either posted on a wall or hidden in the depths of a notebook stored on a shelf. A vision, according to DuFour (2015), poses the following question: "'What must we become in order to accomplish our fundamental purpose?' In pursuing this question, a staff attempts to create a compelling, attractive, realistic future that describes what they hope their school will become" (p. 39). Tim Kanold (2011) writes that "vision, when led extremely well, becomes the driver of change for your district, school, or program area" (p. 11). For schools, the vision almost always has to do with increasing student achievement. A mission is different from a vision, however, because the former defines a school's purpose (DuFour et al., 2016). The school's mission answers why we exist. Schools might exist to provide positive learning environments for all students. This will then lead a school to creating a vision of what the school will need to become in order to make that happen.

Collaborative leaders understand the necessity of not only collectively creating a vision but also ensuring that the vision drives what is happening in a school. Collaborative leaders help create a collective vision perceived as attainable and worth the effort. After all, "most faculty and staff are willing to work hard and go above and beyond what typically might be expected—if they believe the purpose is worthwhile" (Eaker & Keating, 2012, p. 25). DuFour (2015) further emphasizes this when he states that the "power of a vision statement will depend less on its eloquence and more on the degree to which stakeholders throughout the school or district share it and align their collective actions with it" (p. 108).

A correctly executed, agreed-on vision ensures that every goal is focused on it and provides guidance and support for everyone as the leader helps members move through change. Toward that end, collaborative leaders set goals with their teams, establish required actions, and monitor growth—efforts that are covered in chapter 5 (page 53). They can get teams back on course and provide different structures to ensure they're truly working toward the vision. As we see in this chapter, they understand that visioning is a first step in what needs to be a sustainable journey that includes differentiating facts from beliefs, ensuring that the vision is shared, and helping teams commit to the vision. Use the questions in this chapter to examine your beliefs about the visioning process.

EXAMINING YOUR CURRENT REALITY

As you read this chapter, consider the following questions. Reflect on your personal growth as a leader and your support of growing leadership within your organization.

- What are your three strongest beliefs regarding education?
- Where did they come from?
- How do you know they are the right beliefs?
- What are your beliefs about leading an organization focused on student success?
- How do you know those beliefs will make a difference?
- Who is important to include in the visioning process?
- How do you make sure those people are included?
- How pervasive is your vision throughout your school?
- What evidence of the vision is clearly visible?
- How is the vision moving from words to actions?
- What concerns you in regard to buy-in of the vision?

*Visit **go.SolutionTree.com/leadership** for a free reproducible version of this feature box.*

Differentiate Facts From Beliefs

Can you ensure that the vision you are collectively creating is founded on facts instead of assumptions? (See "Facts or Assumptions" on page 50 to help you and your teams discern.) While visions are built on the beliefs of those who create them, we have often found that the beliefs themselves may or may not have been based on factual evidence. You need to take the time to honor each belief, while ensuring that there is evidence to support it; you want data to drive the vision creation (and goals and processes thereafter). For example, the state of South Dakota had fewer than 140,000 students enrolled in its entire K–12 public schools during 2017

(South Dakota Department of Education, n.d.). Illinois has almost 371,000 students enrolled in Chicago public schools alone (Chicago Public Schools, n.d.). Just that one fact could drastically change the way someone understands education in either setting. A large South Dakota high school student body may seem exceptionally large in that state, and administrators could make decisions based on the belief that it is a large high school population, even though it is much smaller than a large high school population in Chicago.

Educators, parents, and even students often deal only in their immediate surroundings. A 2017 American Federation of Teachers national poll shows that almost three-quarters of parents prefer a high-quality neighborhood school to other choices. If a school is in an at-risk area, it is often difficult to see beyond what those students and educators have to deal with every day. This fact highlights how important it is that educators look at comparable educational settings when designing their vision statements in order to better understand what is happening outside their current reality. Educators use this knowledge to see what is working and is not working in other educational settings. They then begin conversations in regard to limitations and expectations. Are they founded in fact or belief? This can be true whether a school is high performing, low performing, or in between.

Develop a Shared Vision

A vision does not necessarily represent a wide group of people, nor does it necessarily reflect the school's direction. An *effective* vision does, however. It is important that all stakeholders be represented when creating the vision. *Stakeholders* are most easily defined as those who will be charged with moving the vision forward. It includes all educators but could also include other staff, parents, and students. Not each of these groups has to help draft the vision, but their voices should be heard when initially addressing the vision, and they are informed along the way. For ease of drafting a vision, include group representatives. These representatives could be grade-level or content-area representatives. Leaders might also wish to include a parent and student representative or two.

A leader who develops a shared vision is ahead of the game. A shared vision automatically grows the efforts of those sharing it. Kanold (2011) further defines this: "All stakeholders must own the vision, and if they don't have a voice in its development, they will never completely honor it" (p. 19). An expansive research review shows that as people participate in developing the vision, "they will assimilate the vision, developing identification with and shared ownership of the vision. Broader participation in the process will have a positive effect on how widely the vision is held" (O'Connell, Hickerson, & Pillutla, 2011, p. 113). Broader participation necessarily means that different, often disparate, interests will be at stake for different groups. Choosing priorities can make emotions run high because, according to professors John Antonakis and Robert Hooijberg (2007), "this is when the consequences of the vision for the team members and company divisions will become apparent." Keeping a common focus on learning, and the fact that everyone is responsible for ensuring that every student learns, will help leaders handle different ideas that come from different groups.

Regarding a school's direction, we believe that learning for all students has to be a key part of any educational vision. Without it, what a school can do is limited. Because collaborative leadership helps a school be the best that it can be, we could not complete this chapter on visioning without some words to that end. At first, a vision can seem unrealistic. Try a "Yes, but" response if you meet resistance. For example, if a teacher says, "We can't expect all students to learn, because some struggle," a committed, effective collaborative leader and his or her team members could reply, "*Yes*, we do have struggling students, *but* we can act to move them out of the struggling category." This answer honors the teacher's feelings and gives him or her more options.

Many books and online resources illustrate the process of creating a vision. It is essential that you find one that promotes a shared visioning process. Because it's such an intensive process, we do not cover it at length here, but we've included action steps for creating a vision later in this chapter (pages 48–49). Protocols from the National School Reform Faculty (Murphy, 2002; www.nsrfharmony.org/system/files/protocols/future.pdf) and Brown University (Clarke, 2003; http://bit.ly/2xStycw) can guide the creation of a team's vision as well. Visit **go.SolutionTree.com/leadership** to access the websites mentioned in this book.

The same category of educational literature and resources is readily available for teams defining the best educational setting possible. At the start, ask yourself what makes a school high achieving regardless of affluence or population and why some schools struggle. Review other schools' visions that have similar current realities. Do not take shortcuts through this process. Be totally transparent with your educational community. Use newsletters and meetings to inform everyone of the process and where you are in it. Continuously gather feedback from key stakeholders and use that to create or adjust next steps.

Help Teams Commit to the Vision

Team commitment starts with collaboratively creating the vision, but it doesn't end there. It is important to use that vision as a guide for teams to create collective commitments. This can be done through answering the following questions: How is each team going to work to further the vision? What actions are team members going to take? How will they hold each other responsible? Eventually, commitment becomes the way team members do their work. The focus shifts from What do we do? to Are we doing enough? But such an environment and a culture are not created overnight. Michael Fullan (2007) warns us that "making a difference in the lives of students requires care, commitment, and passion as well as the intellectual know-how to do something about it" (p. 20).

Not only do effective leaders rally people behind a common cause, but they also support the commitments others are willing to make to promote that cause. For example, a team might commit to aligning standards to assessments. Effective leaders could help get the appropriate professional development or software program, or they could reschedule the day to allow the team more collaboration time. These commitments gather momentum when they are not incumbent on one individual. Team-developed commitments promote individuals supporting each other to ensure adherence to the commitment. Collective commitments and common goals can create a sense of purpose and pride, because "when people have a sense of efficacy and an ability to influence their world, they strive to be productive. They direct their energy and intelligence toward making a contribution" (Bolman & Deal, 2011, pp. 130–131).

Creating a system for identifying and reviewing these commitments provides support and assists with celebrating progress. A guiding coalition tracks progress by establishing team reporting times. This reporting also ensures transparent communication. Begin each year with a time for groups of people to make these collective commitments. These commitments can be of special interest to the group, but they must be aligned with the vision of the school. For example, if a school's vision states that all students will actively engage in their learning, a group might decide to research and develop a way for students to write their own academic goals for success.

Sometimes the best way to begin ensuring that everyone shares in the commitment is to give voice to factors that might be impeding progress. Make time during team meetings for everyone to point out assumptions that might be getting in the way. It might be best to do this anonymously at first. Ask team members to determine what they think might be getting in the way of commitments. Have them post these issues, and then have a discussion about how each issue can be addressed. Heed one word of caution: this entire endeavor's success is directly related to the strength of the leader's belief in and actions around the vision.

Develop Common Goals

Another way to ensure that the vision remains a living document is to break down the agreed-on vision into goals. (See "Moving From One to All," page 51, to move a group's thinking into a usable, consensual format.) A team needs goals that guide its work and show when that work is complete. Though a team may have all types of goals, those that make the biggest difference are directly related to achievement and monitored through student growth. Goals unrelated to student growth might be something related to process for increasing collaboration among team members. These can assist with helping students improve, but they are not directly related. The best way to create goals directly related to student growth or progress is to write SMART goals (O'Neill & Conzemius, 2006), which should be the following.

- **Strategic and specific:** The team's goal aligns with the goals of the school or district.
- **Measurable:** The goal includes quantifiable terms.
- **Attainable:** The team believes the goal is achievable.
- **Results oriented:** The goal requires evidence of improved student learning.
- **Time bound:** The goal will be accomplished within a specific period of time.

When goals are strategic and specific, measurable, attainable, results oriented, and time bound, a collaborative leader can utilize them to both support and monitor the team's work. The goals also help maintain common expectations within and between teams. When set correctly, they reveal the desired end results so members and leaders can accurately create action steps that achieve those results, as well as monitor their progress along the way. (Visit **go.SolutionTree.com/leadership** for action steps for creating and attaining goals, as well as a goal growth chart.)

Strategic and specific goals are written around a defined need and relate directly to the vision. Starting points depend on the school's needs. Teams have greater flexibility when students are already showing success. For example, if the school's student achievement scores are lower than district or state scores, then the immediate need is to improve scores. When creating measurable goals, think about how the school year is structured. Most goals should conclude within a single school year. Team leaders and members work together to make appropriate completion dates. If two or more teams are working toward the same goal, together they should discuss the most appropriate timeframes for completing those goals. Most goals will have multi-step processes, and timeframes for each step help keep things moving forward.

Attainability requires considering context. For example, all teachers should strive for 100 percent success for their students, but if the current success rate is 25 percent, then 100 percent success within one year might be unattainable. A results-bound goal is well defined, which helps identify what data to review and when. Of course, since you are monitoring progress of the goals along the way, you can modify SMART goals and adjust deadlines as it becomes apparent that adjustments are necessary.

Conclusion

In this chapter, we answered the question, How can I help develop a vision? Take time answering the following questions, and think critically about each.

- What are you doing right now that fits with what you learned from reading this chapter?
- What might you stop doing after reading this chapter?
- What might you start doing after reading this chapter?

Action Steps for Beginning to Create a Vision

A vision should promote continuous growth and improvement. The following four steps will involve key stakeholders and create a vision that will enhance your school.

1. As you continue building or refining your school's vision, consider how you can make a clear, compelling case for what you believe should be in the vision. What would resonate with team members and school staff?
   a. Collect regional and national education statistics that reflect your school's demographics, and share with faculty members. You could share this with your entire school community as well (in a newsletter, for instance).
   b. Watch for data trends in your district and your building. Present this information in a format that you can share with appropriate stakeholders. Develop case studies or simple anecdotal pieces that illustrate defined populations in your building. Ensure that the facts are readily available to stakeholders. You could share this in a leader's newsletter to faculty and parents. However, always share positive information when sharing negative information.
   c. Early on, gather stakeholders and use the "Facts or Assumptions" worksheet (page 50) to show how beliefs might be based on facts or assumptions. This will help everyone better understand what the vision should include.
2. Ensure that every voice is heard and valued in the visioning process. Here are four ways to ensure that you gather feedback from every stakeholder.
   a. Establish parent gatherings so you can collect their thoughts. Invite them in for breakfast or lunch at school, or have a parent host.
   b. Converse about the school's vision with the entire faculty. To make it more manageable, you could do this in a small group or with teams of teachers.
   c. Meet with groups that are heavily involved in the school. Any organization that supports the school or its surrounding community could participate. Ask questions and collect the responses as a first step in a visioning process.
      - "What are the three greatest things about our school?"
      - "Five years from now, what do you want people to be saying about our school?"
      - "What do you think students need in order to become successful adults?"

   d. Encourage other ways for everyone to think about what their school or district will look like in the future.
      i. Choose an individual class, grade level, student council group, or music class to prepare a short play for parents, depicting a day in the life of your school ten years in the future.
      ii. Have a group of students write a website article about the school ten years from now.
3. Strategize how to assemble every stakeholder group's thinking into a usable format.
   - When getting large groups of people together, find a way to ensure that everyone gets to speak while you capture common thinking. You can do this by using the "Moving From One to All" activity (page 51).
4. Continue focusing on the positive throughout this process. It is important to celebrate the visioning process all along the way.

Facts or Assumptions

As a part of helping create a vision, it's important to discern between facts and assumptions. Use this seven-step exercise to show how beliefs might be based on facts or assumptions and confirm that data are most important.

1. On a 3 × 5 card, write a statement of belief that guides your work. You may use up to five cards. You might need to prioritize and write only those beliefs that seem most evident.
2. At your table, group like beliefs and be prepared to share with the whole group.
3. Have someone record one belief from each group until all groupings have been shared.
4. Choose a few beliefs and discuss whether they are based on facts supported by data or are merely assumptions.
5. Have each table prioritize its original beliefs, and then decide if there are data or research that support each belief, beginning with the one that takes first priority. You can also do this with the whole group, if time permits.
6. Ask each table to discuss the difference between an environment that is driven by facts and one that is driven by assumptions.
7. Brainstorm ideas for making your school more fact, data, and research based.

Moving From One to All

Use this exercise as a consensus maker. It will help you move a group's thinking into a usable, consensual format.

1. Introduce one defined topic to everyone. "What will our fifth-grade students look like when they are graduating from high school?" is an example.
2. Have individuals write their thinking on 3 × 5 index cards, with one thought per card. Have them write no more than five cards.
3. Have a table of six or fewer people share and group like cards, discuss any that might fit the piles with more than one card, and determine if research backs the thinking.
4. Have each group come up with three to five points that members shared most often.
5. Group two or three tables, and combine the points again to get those most common.
6. Make a group decision regarding how many big ideas or points you want at the end.
7. Use these points to guide the vision development, or include them in the final vision.

....

Topic: ____

Main points from table

1. ____
2. ____
3. ____
4. ____
5. ____

Group big ideas

1. ____
2. ____
3. ____

CHAPTER **FIVE**

How Can I Support Teams?

Collaborative leaders must provide their teams with not only information but also people skills and team tools. Every team has a structure, of course, but specific structures and tools, including team norms, goals, and a collaborative inquiry process are necessary for collaboratively led teams. Not only do these structures assist with the actual work, but they support each team's collaborative nature. Collaborative leaders also continually revisit and revise, when necessary, the structures and tools they have in place.

When they implement identified support structures and tools for each group, leaders can better monitor, support, and celebrate with others and replicate those efforts. These structures and tools enable autonomy while preventing isolation, which is important because:

> Teams of adults cannot be afraid or worried about what will happen if a new idea they decide to try is not working. One way to feel more comfortable with autonomy over how to get things done is to make sure that every risk-taking action is tied back to some aspect of student growth and learning achievement. (Kanold, 2011, p. 49)

Having tools and structures in place that are as simple as meeting agendas or as complex as an agreed-on process for engaging in collective inquiry also assists teams with embracing autonomy. (Read more about autonomy in chapter 3 on page 27.)

As we will explore in this chapter, effective support starts by identifying a common language with which teams communicate their vision and work. That support continues when you provide a meeting time during which teams work together. Also, you can help your teams achieve their goals by creating tools with them (for improving efficiency and recordkeeping, for instance) if such tools don't currently exist. Finally, you can help them focus on curriculum, instruction, and assessment. The action steps (page 63), as well as this chapter's other strategies, help as you support collaborative teams.

EXAMINING YOUR CURRENT REALITY

As you read this chapter, consider the following questions. Reflect on your personal growth as a leader and your support of growing leadership within your organization.

- What team structures are currently in place in your school?
- How do you know they are working?
- What tools do your teams use?
- Who created those tools?
- How do you know all teams are using them?
- How do you monitor team progress toward their goals and toward the vision?
- What do you monitor and how often?
- What products do you find the most valuable?
- How do your teams know that they have done good work?

Visit ***go.SolutionTree.com/leadership*** *for a free reproducible version of this feature box.*

Identify a Common Vocabulary

An often-unaddressed component of team success is ensuring that there is a common vocabulary around the structures of the teams, to ensure that everyone is speaking the same language. With collaborative leadership, a common vocabulary is even more important. Industrial design professors Joyce Thomas and Deana McDonagh (2013) explain why:

> Within the process of collaboration, a shared working language should be developed that helps to define and sometimes redefine terms, language and processes to reduce the need for translation. This agreement is helpful in developing a consistent frame of reference for rigorous expectations. (p. 48)

If someone is talking about team notebooks, for example, a common language ensures that everyone knows what that means, who is a part of them, and why they are necessary. As with vision and goals, creating a common language is most effective when a team creates it together (Thomas & McDonagh, 2013).

Getting small groups of teachers together to write a definition around common terms and then sharing those small-group definitions with the large group can help everyone understand a common meaning of each term. It also often shows how differently people might be defining the term. Creating a common vocabulary for teams is often an ongoing process as the teams themselves emerge and grow.

Find Common Time

Many educators talk about finding time for collaboration. DuFour (2015) speaks to the fact that we should not find time; rather, we should provide time. Examining and blocking out common time for team members is one way to provide that collaboration. Designate times to meet and work. In many schools, the guiding coalition ensures that teams do have the time. You can accomplish this by including late student start times or weekly early release days.

Create Team Tools

When used appropriately, collaboration tools drive momentum. For instance, teams can easily refer to tools such as team agendas, norms, notebooks, and products and share the information to provide the appropriate support and guidance to other team members. Designate a time each year for teams to share what tools they have created. The middle of the year works well because they have had a semester to develop tools and have another semester to adjust and add to them based on what they learn from other teams. They can explain why they created the tools and how they use them. Team-created tools help with monitoring, for they are tangible and show what teams are working on; they reveal what support each team needs as well. It's important to refer to and monitor the team tools; they are not simply part of a checklist.

Team Agendas

Team agendas put forth the topics that members will discuss in a meeting. They can also include a discussion summary, achieved outcomes, and next steps for future meetings, as well as norms or products the team is working on. The agenda keeps everyone on track and helps members efficiently manage their limited time. You can review meeting minutes or agendas to ensure that the work is focused on student learning, to identify gaps, and to discover what additional support teams need. The "Team Agenda and Meeting Minutes" template (page 64), part of the action steps for this chapter, can help you create these tools. Allow teams the autonomy to create agendas that meet their needs as well as systems for creating, monitoring, and following them, as long as the agendas are aligned to the right work.

Team Norms

Team norms provide group governance. *Norms* are common commitments that guide team actions. Having a strong set of team norms helps members understand their commitments to one another, as well as how they will act when they are together. For example, if one norm is to stay focused on the work and the agenda, members commit to spending their valuable time focused on agenda items and to avoiding other possible conversations. The "Creating Team Norms" worksheet (page 65) later in this chapter helps you determine norms with your team. Common examples include coming to meetings on time and eliminating side conversations during the meeting. Conversely, continued conversations, backchannel conversations, or additional side conversations during breaks or outside of the scheduled meeting are productive.

Consider incorporating these norms into team communication. Pentland's (2012) research shows the following.

> Successful teams share several defining characteristics:
>
> 1. Everyone on the team talks and listens in roughly equal measure, keeping contributions short and sweet.
> 2. Members face one another . . .
> 3. Members connect directly with one another—not just with the team leader.
> 4. Members carry on back-channel or side conversations within the team.
> 5. Members periodically break, go exploring outside the team, and bring information back.

Additionally, DuFour et al. (2016) offer the following six tips for creating team norms:

> 1. Each team should create its own norms.
> 2. Norms should be stated as commitments to act or behave in certain ways rather than as beliefs.
> 3. Norms should be reviewed at the beginning and end of each meeting for at least six months.
> 4. Teams should formally evaluate their effectiveness at least twice a year.
> 5. Teams should focus on a few essential norms rather than creating an extensive laundry list.
> 6. One of the team's norms should clarify how the team will respond if one or more members are not observing the norms. (pp. 73–74)

Team norms help maintain trust among the team members, and they promote functional ways to deal with conflict. In fact, research shows that "leaders who held high expectations of such behaviors were able to significantly raise the collaborative problem solving norms established by their teams" (Taggar & Ellis, 2007). When effective norms are in place, team members can disagree with one another respectfully and weigh the evidence of potential changes they need to make to individual and team practices without damaging relationships.

Team Notebooks

Team notebooks contain all documents the team creates. The notebooks can be either electronic or hard copy, as long as past documents are easily accessible. Notebooks can include agendas, norms, SMART goals, essential and priority standard lists, student data for essential standards, and team celebrations. Electronic versions can be, as an example, set up using Google Drive (www.google.com/drive) or intranet folders on the district's network. Designate times throughout and at the end of the year to reflect on the notebooks to celebrate growth and work completion. Guiding coalition members also make notebooks available during meetings.

Team Products

Team products, also referred to as *artifacts*, are concrete evidence toward goals. There is no end to what these categories entail, including the following.

- SMART goals
- Standards documents
- Video clips of instructional strategies
- Formative assessments
- Summative assessments
- Data-analysis documents
- Spreadsheets or graphs illustrating data over time
- Celebration documents

Products are not simply evidence that something was done; they are usable tools. Sharing products and successes accelerates positive results and should occur at monthly staff, guiding coalition, or collaborative team meetings. For example, when a team achieves a SMART goal, members can share the skill they were working on with students, the beginning and current achievement data, and—most important—the strategies that generated the results.

Monitoring these pieces is not equivalent to micromanaging. You are transforming individual teamwork into collective teamwork, thereby educating yourself and furthering your team alignment. One can share this type of data with the guiding coalition or the entire school; the principal can share it with other leaders across the district. This approach ensures that gaps are addressed and that students get what they need both within and across grade levels.

Focus on Curriculum, Instruction, and Assessment

Collaborative leaders take the idea of focusing on learning, make it pervasive throughout the organization, and encourage staff to learn from and with one another. In action, that looks like the elements we have mentioned in this book: staff weighing evidence and engaging in collaborative inquiry; discussing the collective vision; setting goals together to build consensus and commitment; and investigating the best ways to achieve set goals, forming a plan, and adjusting along the way. Research bears out this approach's effectiveness. According to dean of education of Trent University Catherine D. Bruce and research officer Tara Flynn (2013), collaborative inquiry "was found to increase teacher efficacy, student achievement, and positive student beliefs" (p. 691). Therefore, teams' focus should be those things that generate the biggest potential gains. According to preeminent researcher John Hattie (2009), teacher collective efficacy is the most impactful factor influencing student achievement that schools can choose to address. Teacher *efficacy*, or the belief a teacher has what can positively impact student learning, is exceptionally important. We have yet to see a school that generates high levels of learning over a sustained period of time that does not have staff that fit this mold.

Some leaders go as far as to challenge members to come up with a unique way to address a situation based on the improvement for which they are searching. Is it a quicker way? Is it a more systematic way? Does it involve more people? There are all sorts of ways to improve. As Hattie (2009) illuminates in his book *Visible Learning*, almost any implemented educational practice that positively affects student achievement will work to some degree. There are very few strategies that would have a negative impact on student learning. We agree with Hattie that the first consideration should be the effect's magnitude.

We like the efficacy shown by asking the four critical questions of the PLC process (DuFour et al., 2016).

1. What do we expect students to learn?
2. How will we know if they have learned these things?
3. How will we respond when some students are not learning?
4. How will we respond when some students already know the content?

These questions engage staff in the kind of collaborative inquiry previously discussed and frame investigating what will generate results for students.

How do collaborative leaders support teams in this effort? By keeping them focused on the right work. When teams focus on the right work, collaborative leaders are mostly monitoring curriculum, instruction, and assessment. As an example, if the school leadership team notices low performance with third graders and wonders about the K–3 curriculum, it could review the kindergarten, first-, and second-grade curricula to discover how it impacted third-grade test scores. Or a guiding coalition could, upon finding a high student absence rate, change instructional practices to increase student engagement and increase student attendance as a result. Yet another school leader could review and change assessment practices so students have more ways to show what they know, thereby increasing their achievement scores. Supporting team curriculum, instruction, and assessment work is covered in the following sections.

Curriculum

An extensive research base addresses the importance of establishing the content teachers should address with students and the time necessary to do so—research that dates back to the effective schools movement in the late 1970s and early 1980s. Ron Edmonds's (1979) seminal article "Effective Schools for the Urban Poor" highlights six correlates of effective schools based upon research. One of those correlates was basic school skills taking precedence over other activities—in other words, valuing the curriculum. This remains on the list of almost all school improvement models today. For example, Marzano's high reliability schools model includes an entire level on establishing a guaranteed and viable curriculum (Marzano, Warrick, & Simms, 2014).

Instruction

If schools decide to begin their work on instruction, a leader's first step is to establish, with the entire school staff, a model for instruction or what they believe great teaching looks like for their school. The school as a whole would develop a common language around the instructional model, identify elements to work on, and utilize better teaching strategies. Leaders can support this work by tapping into one such model, presented by Robert J. Marzano (2017) in *The New Art and Science of Teaching*, which highlights forty-three elements and over three hundred research-based instructional strategies. The task is not finding information *on* instruction but deciding what work to do *around* instruction (and the most effective way to do it). An abundance of instruction resources is available, but the challenge is deciding how the resources correlate to the vision and goals.

Assessment

Assessment is the last area of focus collaborative teams may find a priority. Leaders support assessment work by ensuring all staff understand what quality assessments look like and that teams are effectively using assessments with students. Because assessments confirm actual learning and higher-level thinking (not simply memorization), some schools are still in the process of moving beyond the likes of multiple-choice tests. Increased rigor requires more in-depth thinking and, as a result, higher-level thinking assessment questions. In his book *Making Classroom Assessments Reliable and Valid*, Marzano (2018) makes the case that teacher-created assessments can achieve validity and reliability. In this approach, teachers record *formative* scores (which adjust teaching) and *summative* scores (which address a student's current knowledge or skill level). How teachers use the results, rather than *when* the assessment occurs, determines whether the score is formative or summative.

We would be remiss not to discuss common formative assessments as evidence that the right work is being accomplished. Collaborative teams create assessments to ensure each team member assesses students the same way (known as *common formative assessment*). They give formative assessments more frequently, so they can adapt and change instruction to ensure that learning is occurring for all students. As DuFour, DuFour, Eaker, and Karhanek (2010) emphasize, common formative assessments serve many purposes, including ensuring that all team members have a common definition of student success, comparing student results, discussing strategies that helped students learn (and strategies that didn't), and engaging in collective inquiry. Using common formative assessments can be a powerful vehicle toward improving student achievement.

Examine Data

Data are necessary in many situations, including when comparing your current reality to your vision, when setting goals, at the beginning and end of units of instruction, and prior to celebrations. You can help decide what data to review and ask questions around them. For example, you might have the team look at attendance data if the attendance rate in the school is lower than in surrounding schools. You could, as another example, ask a third-grade team to examine student proficiency data for the standard requiring students to identify a story's main idea. An algebra team might need to examine student proficiency data on polynomials comprehension.

Teams should then ask, "Why?" Authors Laura Lipton and Bruce Wellman (2012) discuss this as part of their collaborative learning cycle, when educators specifically question data in order to dig deeper. The team might ask why their school's attendance data are lower or question what caused the data to look like they do. Questions like these help teams decide whether to address an issue. After examining the attendance data, teams may find that students are not engaged in school, so teams may ask themselves, "What instructional practices can we change to increase student engagement?" When the third-grade team examines data on the main idea standard, it might discover teachers were providing more scaffolding during instruction (by giving students answer choices) than they did on the assessment (by asking students to state the main idea on their own). Finally, the algebra team might find that data vary among team members because some ran out of time and were unable to fully instruct on polynomials.

Regardless of whether the focus is on curriculum, instruction, or assessment, the correct data are important for making informed decisions. Former assistant superintendent Sharon Kramer (2015) states, "Turning data into usable information that can be acted on in a timely manner is what improves schools" (p. 29).

To find evidence that the right work is being done—work that supports high levels of learning for all students—you and your teams must delineate data that illustrate this success. This could be existing data that you track over time, the new data you need, or a combination of both. For example, consider a goal that centers on more students passing an existing end-of-semester exam; measuring growth toward that goal may require both a pretest and incremental formative assessments. With members, decide whether evidence will be quantitative or qualitative. Will the team present assessment results or a narrative documenting what changes occurred? Does it need to create a document that provides the evidence? Will the evidence be first seen in teacher practice and later shown in student work? The relevant questions that leaders can ask teachers or teams are plentiful.

Monitor Work

You can also help teams stay focused by monitoring progress. Establish routine check-ins and regular meetings. You may ask teams to provide documentation showing evidence of their work and the results they have seen. In addition, you can review the natural products that the team creates as a result of doing the work. Ensure that team members understand that you and team leaders are not trying to catch people not doing the work; you are only trying to ensure that the work happens and that you can close any gaps in the work with guidance and support. Use the "Team Monitoring" worksheet (page 39) to accomplish this.

Conclusion

In this chapter, we answered the question, How can I support teams? Take time answering the following questions, and think critically about each.

- What are you doing right now that fits with what you learned from reading this chapter?
- What might you stop doing after reading this chapter?
- What might you start doing after reading this chapter?

Action Steps for Supporting Collaborative Teams

These five action steps will help you identify the tools that teams are using and tools they might need.

1. Review with your teams which tools are currently in place.
    - In each meeting, the team lists the tools it uses.
    - Team leaders bring the lists to a meeting and discuss each tool's value.
    - Team leaders explain any tools that are unique to their team.
    - Determine which, if any, of the tools should be used by all teams.
    - Discuss if there are additional tools that teams might need and, if so, how to obtain or create them.
2. Discuss the necessity of using agendas for every team meeting.
    - An agenda, such as the "Team Agenda and Meeting Minutes" template (page 64), can also serve as a document for creating meeting minutes. Create—or work with team leaders to create—an agenda that has all the components that team leaders want to monitor and use.
3. Have teams use the "Creating Team Norms" worksheet (page 65). Monitor to ensure that teams follow the norms.
4. With teams, decide how to collect and keep important team documents: digitally, hard copy, or both? Base your decision on what is most accessible to team members during their meeting.
5. Celebrate team and school progress.
    - Have teams display their products and artifacts. Conduct a walkthrough where all teams can view one another's products and artifacts.

Team Agenda and Meeting Minutes

This template can serve as a starting point for creating meeting minutes, which is a crucial part of supporting teams. Create—or work with team leaders to create—an agenda that has all the components that team leaders want to monitor and use.

Team name: ____________________ Date: __________ Recorder: ____________________
Day's goal:
Data to use:
Discussion:
Outcomes:
Next steps and person responsible:
Recorder for next time: ____________________

Creating Team Norms

Team norms provide group governance. Helping establish norms and monitoring team members' adherence to them are crucial parts of supporting teams. Follow these seven steps to help establish norms.

1. Give each team member about six sticky notes.
2. Give team members five minutes to identify norms and write them on the sticky notes.
3. Put all the sticky notes in the middle of a table.
4. Give the team fifteen minutes to group the sticky notes in silence.
5. Give the team twenty minutes to discuss groupings and prioritize norms.
6. Write prioritized norms on chart paper to post during team meetings.
7. For durability, laminate the resulting norms document.

CHAPTER **SIX**

What, When, and How Should I Communicate?

There is no doubt that communication is the true key to unlocking doors. Communicating is what we do to ensure that others know what we are thinking. We talk. We gesture. We emote. We continuously strive to get our thoughts and feelings across to others. Trust, empathy, and accessibility all play a part here. After all, "exceptional leaders understand that leadership is not facilitating a series of activities, but rather guiding and encouraging *people* on the journey" (Erkens, 2008, p. 40). Research shows, in fact, that human-oriented leadership, which is "mainly communicative," is strongly related to "perceived leader performance, satisfaction with the leader, [and] subordinates' commitment" (de Vries, Bakker-Pieper, & Oostenveld, 2010, p. 370). The action steps later in this chapter help as you're creating a communication plan (pages 75–76).

Leaders in schools have to transmit information, but schools in particular rely on communication based on connection and inspiration. Collaborative leaders understand that focusing on the positive, regardless of the situation, can more often than not result in a positive outcome. Kouzes and Posner (2011) state, "When leaders are encouraging, others follow their example and organizations develop a reputation for being great places to work" (p. 316). Recognizing growth or movement in a positive direction does more to move an organization forward than trying to change something that is not working. No success is too small to acknowledge.

Ensuring all stakeholder group representatives is a crucial element of communication, too. One way you can ensure complete representation and obtain the evidence of such is by creating a plan that shows the lines of communication. The "Our Way of Communicating" worksheet (page 78) provides schools and teams with a visual representation of how they include all stakeholders. In the Why column, indicate what part, organization, or group requires representation. In the Who column, list all stakeholders involved or impacted by the work teams have identified. In the What column, explain what will be communicated to the stakeholder in the Who column. In the How and When column, explain whether communication will be written or oral and how often it will be communicated. In the From column, record who is responsible for communicating to the entity in the Who column. Not everyone has to involve him- or herself in all work, but clarity about who needs to know what, and how that will happen, will, again, help ensure diverse representation.

That being said, Jim Collins (2001), in his epic book *Good to Great*, has an entire chapter on confronting brutal facts. He writes about company failure due to the lack of culture that would have allowed for both the good and the bad to be communicated and heard. Such a culture would have enabled more honest conversations and better clarity as to the current reality. As schools move along on this journey, it is crucial to listen to all stakeholders, discuss concerns, and work through them. This keeps everyone on the same page and ultimately leads to greater strides toward a sustainable vision.

We begin this chapter discussing the importance of listening to others. We then explore the importance of sharing with others, specifically a variety of stakeholders with whom the sharing of information is important. We conclude with a brief look at the importance of celebrating others, as good communication can always be cause for celebration.

EXAMINING YOUR CURRENT REALITY

As you read this chapter, consider the following questions. Reflect on your personal growth as a leader and your support of growing leadership within your organization.

- What are your current modes of communication?
- What mode do you use most frequently?
- What do you think is the most effective?
- With whom do you think communication is most important and why?
- How could you expand your current communication?
- How could you expand your oral communication?
- How could you expand your written communication?

Visit ***go.SolutionTree.com/leadership*** *for a free reproducible version of this feature box.*

Listen to Others

It is important for collaborative leaders to not only listen but really hear what others are saying. Collaborative leaders, who truly understand people, recognize that there is often more to the message being relayed than the words that are being used to relay it. We have found that people don't just speak in the here and now. They speak from a combination of past, present, and even perceived future experiences. Hear the words *and* understand the messages behind them. People usually do not separate their emotions from the words they are saying. Lipton and Wellman (2012) speak to this when they talk about team dialogue: "Skilled listeners attend to the message behind the words with a desire to understand frames of reference, underlying emotions and assumptions" (p. 80).

It is often helpful to understand *why* someone is communicating as much as to hear *what* he or she is saying. Is it just a matter of needing to vent? Is it a message to be shared with others? Is it just the need to be heard? If a teacher is sharing information about the behavior of a student with whom he or she is struggling, the answer could be yes to any or all of those questions. By taking the time to gather additional information from the person who is communicating, you can often provide better support. One of the best ways to do this is by asking clarifying questions. Work toward clarity; avoid judgment. Simple questions such as How can I help? and What can I do for you? often help provide further information.

Along these same lines, it is also important that you know what to do with the shared information. Sometimes the information does not need to go any further. Other times, you may need to share it as a mandated reporter or with central office leadership. If the information must be shared, it is always best to inform the person sharing the information that this will happen.

Good collaborative leaders often use what they hear to inform and strengthen their own message. Leadership expert and Korn Ferry Institute CEO Gary Burnison (2012) furthers his message on communication by recommending that you "honor the knowledge experts on your team and throughout the organization by seeking out their input and their opinions" (p. 160). Encourage others to share, and enable them to appropriately respond to what they hear. To do this they have to understand what they hear, know why they are hearing it, and put it into a context that leads to a positive outcome for everyone. As a collaborative leader, you might have to facilitate that process. Explaining what you do when you receive information from others is one facilitation method.

Diverse representation is important, as we explained in chapter 3 (page 27). With so many voices wanting to be heard, a framework (such as the communication plan on page 77), along with established parameters, is necessary. The flow of communication needs to run from team to team and back again. Establish this flow, and make it transparent to everyone involved. Answer these questions: Who is going to talk with whom? When is this going to occur? What form will the communication take? How will information be gathered and final decisions shared? The environment of a particular school or setting often influences the answers.

You reap the best results by using the team's expertise to determine how this works best in an individual setting. The teams themselves can brainstorm and help create the appropriate structure for healthy communication. One way to visually depict this is by labeling each end of foot-long pieces of conduit or other pipe. Label one end *LT* for leadership team, and label the other end *CT* for collaborative teams. The teams try to connect all the pipes to see if there are any gaps and if too many people were communicating to the same team. The activity's value comes from ensuring proper communication pieces.

Share With Others

Regardless of what you're communicating about, it is helpful to use multiple configurations, including one-to-one, team and faculty, parent, and student communication. During the time we have been educators and have worked with educators, we have seen a lot of wonderful strategies used to promote communication. We share them with you in the following sections.

One-to-One Communication

There are many ways for leaders to communicate within a school community, but probably the most powerful is face-to-face, one-to-one communication, which research confirms: "The most valuable form of communication is face-to-face . . . 35% of the variation in a team's performance can be accounted for simply by the number of face-to-face exchanges among team members" (Pentland, 2012). This type of communication is extremely impactful for a few reasons. First, it is easier to focus on an individual's concerns. Second, answering questions, addressing concerns, responding to suggestions, and having quality dialogue are easiest when fewer people are involved. Once communication is occurring in a larger-group setting, it is more challenging to ensure that everyone is heard and that the back-and-forth dialogue that is necessary for good communication occurs. The larger a group becomes, the greater the challenge.

Though one-to-one communication is the most impactful, it is also the most time consuming because you're conveying or receiving information from a singular person instead of a collective group. Use this format when opportunities arise. Use it intentionally when contentious situations develop, when there is a lot of potential emotion involved, when the seriousness of the communication and those affected warrants it, and when you need to make progress.

Despite the time required, effective collaborative leaders expand the amount of one-to-one communication that can occur in a school or district. When a school promotes a team of leaders, it can hear more people individually, because that communication doesn't rely on one or two individual leaders. Accomplishing this leadership growth requires many of the elements that we have referred to in previous chapters, including having a high level of trust, being clear on the vision, and focusing on the right work.

Team and Faculty Communication

Traditionally, monthly faculty meetings were the educational setting for learning and leading. Promoting leadership skills in others goes far beyond that, however. Faculty meetings remain a great way to model leadership skills and enable others to showcase theirs, but those meetings are just the beginning.

Collaborative team meetings, vertical team meetings, committee meetings, guiding coalition meetings, and informal conversations between staff members can occur multiple times per day. All of these are great opportunities to promote leadership in others and help them hone their communication skills. Approach these types of meetings as opportunities for open communication. Use them as opportunities to grow other leaders, by giving others the opportunities to create agendas, give presentations, and guide others in their thinking.

Communication is not necessarily synonymous only with meetings, however. Incorporate written communication as well. Weekly newsletters and email updates might include updates and a calendar of upcoming events and meetings, ensuring that everyone has the information they need as soon as they need it. Communication with the school team and faculty is a vital ingredient for building or maintaining a positive school culture. The messages that are communicated, the shifts or continuation of the work that occurs in a school, and the positive things that are recognized and celebrated all help build a school culture. Without consistent high-quality communication, it is much more difficult to build a culture that consistently prioritizes the opening of doors for students.

Parent Communication

Don't fall into the trap of one-way communication with parents. Newsletters, announcements, automated phone calls, agenda books, and Twitter are useful tools, but they lack the reciprocity required for parents to truly understand the work that you and your collaborators are doing to support the vision.

The reality is that all parents went to school. As a result, they often have preconceived notions about what school should look like, sound like, and feel like. Some of these notions are likely accurate, while others could be counterproductive to the mission of the school. Some parents might challenge the idea that all teachers in a course or grade level should be discussing their child's progress, due to the vision they have of what education is. Explaining why collaboration is so important and why it works is key to forging quality relationships with parents. There are many ways to effectively accomplish this type of communication.

One way is to establish town-hall-type meetings. Town hall meetings are opportunities for members of the school community to ask questions and receive responses from school leaders. This is a valuable opportunity for two-way, productive communication. Town hall meetings can be useful if your school is embarking on any sort of change in practice that affects parents and the community, and to periodically connect and garner feedback from the school community.

In promoting a more informal or intimate approach, consider holding coffee hours. These allow smaller groups of parents to get together. You can host them in a variety of neighborhoods or demographic areas. These are ideal for unscripted dialogue around any topic. They also facilitate your understanding the feelings parents might have toward a certain school practice or change.

Focus groups consist of a small but diverse group of constituents who agree to discuss and react to plans the school might be considering. Since a focus group is smaller, it gives school leaders the opportunity to discuss with parents in a more interactive way any possible changes that might need to be made. It also provides a good venue for school leaders to hear parental concerns and thoughts in a less threatening environment. Focus groups are very valuable when considering a second-order change, or a change that breaks with traditional notions of schooling.

Sometimes it is good to invite all parents to certain events, such as town halls or coffee with the principal-type meetings. In this way, they all feel as though they are hearing the same information and that they are a part of the school. Action-oriented activities are helpful. For example, include everyone by putting up posters with different decades or a time the school has been open. Have parents stand by the poster that represents when they first got involved with the school. Have each group at each poster write one major event that occurred during that time period. This celebrates the school's history and helps you know parents better. Not only do these types of activities increase communication, but they are another way to increase understanding and support.

Student Communication

We have spent a lot of time talking about how collaborative leaders promote leadership in others. They can do the same for students, and communication is a great first step. Students need to hear what roles they can play in communication.

Involve students, much like you do parents, by forming focus groups to listen to student needs and concerns. Students can lead these groups and teacher leaders can monitor them. The group members can be self-selected or teacher nominated, dependent on the outcomes you are striving to achieve. If there is a particular goal in mind, you might want to have a specific representation of the student body on the team. Create student leadership teams to spread messages to other students. Hold assemblies and other large-group gatherings so all students hear the same messages. You can help students find their own voices. Involve them in the learning process, so that they themselves can articulate what is happening in their educational environment. On a broader scale, students can discuss school processes, goals, and the current reality. On a more individual level, they know what they are learning, where they are in regard to the learning targets, and what they need to do to move forward. Not only do they know these things, they can communicate them to others.

Celebrate Others

Celebrations are far too infrequent. Leaders tend to focus on celebrating outcomes and forget to champion the progress. Help others feel positive about the sometimes tiring, relentless work they do. Celebrations actually do so much more. Author Anthony Muhammad (2017) asserts, "Celebration in school provides consistent reinforcement about what is important" (p. 126).

Celebrations can take many forms by praising groups (see "Our School's Strengths," page 79, and "Sharing and Celebrating Our Work," pages 80 and 81) and individuals (see "Here's to You," page 83). Create established celebration rituals weekly, monthly, quarterly, and yearly. It helps create a chart, visible to everyone, that highlights what you celebrate—attendance, achievement, birthdays, or leadership skills, for example. The chart should also let people know when the celebrations are taking place. Last, show how you are planning on celebrating—a pat on the back, a free homework pass, or a schoolwide assembly, for example.

By ensuring that celebration is about growth and not always an end goal, you expand the opportunities for individuals to be a part of the positivity. Celebrating growth is also important to student celebrations. The focus need not always be on the end goal, but on the benchmarks of success that occur as a student moves toward that goal. You can also expand the number of celebrations that take place. It takes a little extra work, but it is worth doing everything possible to be sure all members of the educational environment can participate at some point in time.

Conclusion

In this chapter, we answered the question, What, when, and how should I communicate? Take time answering the following questions, and think critically about each.

- What are you doing right now that fits with what you learned from reading this chapter?
- What might you stop doing after reading this chapter?
- What might you start doing after reading this chapter?

Action Steps for Creating a Communication Plan

This plan ensures clear communication about issues important to everyone. Use the six steps in this document with teams when an outcome is to include others in knowing what is being accomplished and why.

1. Take one new idea that the school would like to work on. This is typically about an effort that will impact the entire school. These ideas might have emerged from goal setting exercises or school or team meetings.
   - Establish a solid rationale for why the school wants to try it. One question to ask is, "What data do we have to support this action?"
   - Make clear any changes that will occur.
2. Think about whom the decision will impact.
   - List all stakeholder groups and whether the impact will be small or large. Rate the impact: 1 is no impact or very small impact, 2 is small impact, 3 is medium impact, and 4 is large impact.
   - Discuss with the team the key messages to communicate with each stakeholder group.
3. Teams gather feedback from others, especially the groups who will experience a medium or large impact.
   - Use the "Communication Plan" worksheet (page 77) to specify who needs what communication and other details.
   - Use the "Our Way of Communicating" worksheet (page 78) to create a visual representation that includes all stakeholders.
   - Share with key stakeholders and get their opinions.
   - Debrief as a leadership team to consider all perspectives, and anticipate challenges to the implementation.
4. Establish periodic meeting times for the group to come back together and report on progress. Also, use this time to address any concerns or voice any positives that have occurred.
   - Gather feedback from multiple stakeholder groups regarding the implementation.
   - List the positives and negatives associated with people's perception of the change.
5. After implementing the change, return to the chart. Are there any gaps in the communication plan? Use this information to plan for the next time.

page 1 of 2

6. With your leadership team, the team that is a conduit for all other teams, decide how to publicly celebrate individual or group successes. The leadership team might choose to get ideas from the other teams they represent. You could use faculty meetings, newsletters, staff updates, or bulletin boards as a time or place. Consider using the "Our School's Strengths" (page 79) or the "Sharing and Celebrating Our Work" worksheets (page 80).
   a. Early in the process of promoting collaborative leadership, ask others for their input on what should be recognized in order to show growth in the process.
   b. Use the "Leading a Celebration" worksheet (page 79) to list no more than seven items on which you wish to focus and celebrate growth this year. Decide how often—weekly, monthly, quarterly, or yearly—you are going to recognize achievement on each item.
   c. During an established time, such as a faculty meeting, go through the "Leading a Celebration" worksheet and mark each item with *B* for beginning, *I* for implementing, or *S* for sustaining.
   d. Use the worksheet and "Here's to You" (pages 83 and 84) to guide your focus prior to the next meeting.
   e. At the end of the year, celebrate the growth that has occurred and is documented on the chart.
   f. Ask others what the celebration should be—such as treats in the lounge, gifts for the teachers, recognition in a parent newsletter, and so on.

Communication Plan

Collaborative leaders use communication to relay information, to connect, and to inspire. Plan in advance who needs what communication, how and when it should be transmitted, and who will convey it.

Date: ______________________________

Who needs it?	What do they need?	How should we do it?	Who will be responsible?	When will communication occur?
Central office				
Building administrators				
Teachers				
Students				
Parents				
Community at large				
Other:				

Title of what needs to be communicated: ______________________________

Our Way of Communicating

In the Why column, indicate what part, organization, or group requires representation. In the Who column, list all stakeholders involved or impacted by the work teams have identified. In the What column, explain what will be communicated to the stakeholder in the Who column. In the How and When column, explain whether communication will be written or oral and how often it will be communicated. Some examples include quantitative data changes, anecdotal, and other information regarding needs, progress, or celebrations. In the From column, record who is responsible for communicating to the entity in the Who column.

School or district name: ______________________________

Why	Who	What	How and When	From

Our School's Strengths

Celebrate teams for achieving short- and long-term work toward goals by completing this form and posting it in a prominent agreed-on place, such as a lounge bulletin board.

This week: ____________________________________

At our school: ____________________________________

This happened: ____

____

____

____

____

____

____

____

____

____

Congratulations to these people for helping make it happen: _____________

____

____

____

____

____

Sharing and Celebrating Our Work

Celebrate teams for achieving short- and long-term work toward goals by completing this form and posting it in a prominent agreed-on place, such as a lounge bulletin board.

District or school: ______________________________

Date: ____________________

Team:

Quantitative results—We documented the following:

Data type:

Circle the one for which you are striving: Increase in data or Decrease in data

Comments		
	Teacher teams	
	Students	
	Other	

Qualitative results—We observed, felt, or heard the following:

Group observed:

Comments	
Teacher teams	
Students	
Other	

What we learned:

What we plan to do next:

Leading a Celebration

List seven or fewer topics on which you wish to focus and celebrate growth for this year. Decide how often—weekly, monthly, quarterly, or yearly—you are going to recognize achievement for each topic. Mark each item with *B* for beginning (introducing the idea and gathering support for it), *I* for implementing (celebrating and making adjustments as needed), or *S* for sustaining (having it ingrained in the school culture).

Topic	Weekly	Monthly	Quarterly	Yearly

Here's to You

This celebration activity is one way to highlight individual leadership. It promotes a way for recognition to come from peers, not just from leadership. Anyone can fill out a recognition document for anyone in the district.

You can use this same type of activity to praise teams. Team celebrations can be exclusive to the team and created by it—for example, "Congratulations to us for adhering to our norms today!" Leadership as a whole can find ways to celebrate teams more publicly. Consider the following four steps.

1. Make copies of the following "Here's to You" sheet (page 84) on colored sheets of paper.
2. Put the copies in a place that is easy for teachers to access.
3. Introduce this strategy at a faculty meeting with the following directions.
    - Anytime you see another teacher or adult in our building doing something to help lead us in the right direction, please take a "Here's to You" sheet and complete it.
    - Put the completed sheets in a designated place to be read aloud during future faculty meetings.
4. Follow through by reading the sheets aloud at a faculty meeting. The building leader can initiate the process by completing a few sheets or encouraging others to do so.

Here's to You

Here's to ____ for providing leadership by . . .

Here's to You

Here's to ____ for providing leadership by . . .

EPILOGUE
Concluding Thoughts

Richard DuFour's (2015) *In Praise of American Educators* is both a celebration of educators and a call to continue strengthening the education system. He summed up so much of what we have written and expounded on in this book with this statement:

> American schools need principals who have the courage to move beyond managing to leading and developing the leadership capacity of many others, principals who can build consensus for substantive change and work through the inevitable discomfort, and principals who accept there will be times when they must settle for less than universal affection from their staff. Those who take this path less chosen will embrace and articulate the moral imperative of ensuring high levels of learning for all students and will acknowledge that creating the conditions for addressing that imperative lies within their sphere of influence. (p. 247)

From looking internally at what a collaborative leader knows and does, to externally building structures and support systems, you can see that your work is unique. In this book, we have talked about the work that is critical to schools (see the "One Big Thing" worksheet on page 88) and how your collaborative leadership is critical to that work. However, like so many things that occur in education, this work needs appropriate care and feeding. We would like you to reflect on what you have learned and plan for action ahead. One way to do this is by following the action steps for leading the right work (page 87) and another way is by using the "Where's My Thinking?" worksheet (page 89).

Again, it doesn't take a special person to become a collaborative leader, but it does take integrity and empathy. Maybe the best thing about all of this is that it is not about going out and learning something new. It is about understanding yourself as a leader, about the freedom to know that you do not have to lead alone, and about structuring leadership tasks that promise to be more effective. It is about taking what you know has worked and supporting others to join in the work—not for the sake of doing the work but because you and the others know that by your doing so, success can multiply.

We have quoted Jim Collins (2001) previously. He speaks of many of the qualities we find in collaborative leaders. These are strong leaders willing to take responsibility, not place blame, and always give credit where credit is due:

> Leaders look out the window to apportion credit to factors outside themselves when things go well (and if they cannot find a specific person or event to give credit to, they credit good luck). At the same time, they look in the mirror to apportion responsibility, never blaming bad luck when things go poorly. (p. 35)

Economist Herminia Ibarra (2015) speaks to many years of research when she states, "Inevitably, the researchers discover that effective leaders are highly self-aware, purpose-driven, and authentic" (p. 3). The world of education is in need of such leaders. It needs leaders who will connect with their teachers or principals and bring out their best; leaders who will create safe, dynamic learning environments where students can succeed; leaders who actively explore and nourish their own growth. Leaders such as this will carry our schools forward. We hope this book has helped bring out that leader in you.

EXAMINING YOUR CURRENT REALITY

As you finish this book, consider the following questions. Reflect on your personal growth as a leader and your support of growing leadership within your organization.

- What makes you a collaborative leader?
- What are your strengths in this regard?
- What would others say about you?
- What do you need to do to be a continuously improving leader?
- What help do you need from others?
- Where can you seek resources to help you grow?
- How are you continuously growing and supporting others?
- What actions do you take?

Visit ***go.SolutionTree.com/leadership*** *for a free reproducible version of this feature box.*

Action Steps for Leading the Right Work

This twelve-step activity is a comprehensive way to focus the educators in your building on a single area of growth. By first looking at the data historically, educators can understand why the data look the way they do. All teams throughout the building can then build their goals from the findings.

1. Determine an area of emphasis or improvement on which you wish to focus.
2. Review information or data about your school or district for the past five years. The data could be from local newspapers (even past school newsletters), or they could be achievement data posted by the state or district.
3. Look for common data, and assess trending information. Make sure that it is an area of multiyear growth.
4. Share no more than three pieces of data with the school or district.
5. Create a graphic around that data, and provide room to speculate on what will happen in the next couple of years. Use these speculations to help maintain focus in the first year of promoting leadership in others.
6. If you deem it appropriate, share your conclusions with others by including them in the faculty and parent newsletters.
7. Have your leadership team use the data to form appropriate school-level plans involving curriculum, instruction, and assessment.
8. Use the "One Big Thing" worksheet (page 88) with your teams to help decide on a single focus. Make sure that the focus is directly tied to improving student learning.
9. Create a specific timeline of data checks and benchmarks for this work so you can monitor growth. Decide what and when to monitor, and keep up with the timeline.
10. As a school, reflect on how well the plans are working, what adjustments to make, and how the staff as a whole knows this is the right work.
11. Arrange a time when each team can share the following.
    - What they are working on
    - What they are learning
    - What they plan to do next
12. Between those times that each team shares, talk about how the shared information might impact other teams or the staff as a whole.

One Big Thing

Use this worksheet with your teams to help decide what your single focus will be. Make sure that the focus is directly tied to improving student learning.

Team: ______________________________

Date: ______________________________

What one thing could we change that would improve student outcomes?

What resources do we need in order to accomplish it?

What action steps will we take to accomplish it?

What evidence will show that we accomplished it?

Where's My Thinking?

Use this worksheet to reflect personally on what you have learned about collaborative leadership and what your plans are.

Originally, I was thinking . . .

Then I learned . . .

Now, my thinking is . . .

I will consider these future thoughts . . .

REFERENCES AND RESOURCES

American Federation of Teachers. (2017, September 12). *National poll finds parents want safe, welcoming, well-funded neighborhood public schools; overwhelmingly support public schools* [Press release]. Accessed at www.aft.org/press-release/national-poll-finds-parents-want-safe-welcoming-well-funded-neighborhood on January 29, 2018.

Antonakis, J., & Hooijberg, R. (2007). Cascading vision for real commitment. In R. Hooijberg, J. G. Hunt, J. Antonakis, K. B. Boal, & N. Lane (Eds.), *Being there even when you are not: Leading through strategy, structures, and systems* (pp. 231–244). Amsterdam: Elsevier Science.

Bachelder, C. (2015). *Dare to serve: How to drive superior results by serving others.* Oakland, CA: Berrett-Koehler.

Barlow, V. E. (2001). *Trust and the principalship.* Unpublished manuscript, University of Calgary, British Columbia. Accessed at http://citeseerx.ist.psu.edu/viewdoc/download?doi=10.1.1.520.6498&rep=rep1&type=pdf on October 30, 2017.

Barrick, M. R., & Mount, M. K. (1991). The big five personality dimensions and job performance: A meta-analysis. *Personnel Psychology, 44*(1), 1–26. doi:10.1111/j.1744-6570.1991.tb00688.x

Barth, R. S. (2003). *Lessons learned: Shaping relationships and the culture of the workplace.* Thousand Oaks, CA: Corwin Press.

Blase, J., & Blase, J. R. (2001). *Empowering teachers: What successful principals do* (2nd ed.). Thousand Oaks, CA: Corwin Press.

Block, P. (2013). *Stewardship: Choosing service over self-interest* (2nd ed.). San Francisco: Berrett-Koehler.

Bolman, L. G., & Deal, T. E. (2011). *Leading with soul: An uncommon journey of spirit* (3rd ed.). San Francisco: Jossey-Bass.

Brewster, C., & Railsback, J. (2003). *Building trusting relationships for school improvement: Implications for principals and teachers.* Portland, OR: Northwest Regional Educational Laboratory. Accessed at http://educationnorthwest.org/sites/default/files/trust.pdf on October 19, 2017.

Bruce, C. D., & Flynn, T. (2013). Assessing the effects of collaborative professional learning: Efficacy shifts in a three-year mathematics study. *Alberta Journal of Educational Research, 58*(4), 691–709. Accessed at www.researchgate.net/publication/261875790_Bruce_C_Flynn_T_2013_Assessing_the_Effects_of_Collaborative_Professional_Learning_Efficacy_shifts_in_a_three-year_mathematics_study_Alberta_Journal_of_Educational_Research_584_691-709 on February 2, 2018.

Bryk, A. S., & Schneider, B. (2002). *Trust in schools: A core resource for improvement.* New York: Russell Sage Foundation.

Buckingham, M. (2005). *The one thing you need to know. . . about great managing, great leading, and sustained individual success.* New York: Free Press.

Buffum, A., Mattos, M., & Weber, C. (2012). *Simplifying response to intervention: Four essential guiding principles.* Bloomington, IN: Solution Tree Press.

Burnison, G. (2012). *The twelve absolutes of leadership.* New York: McGraw-Hill.

Canfield, J. (2005). *The success principles: How to get from where you are to where you want to be.* New York: HarperCollins.

Cashman, K. (2014, March 17). Return on self-awareness: Research validates the bottom line of leadership development. *Forbes.* Accessed at www.forbes.com/sites/kevincashman/2014/03/17/return-on-self-awareness-research-validates-the-bottom-line-of-leadership-development/#741464f63750 on October 23, 2017.

Chicago Public Schools. (n.d.). *CPS stats and facts.* Accessed at https://cps.edu/About_CPS/At-a-glance/Pages/Stats_and_facts.aspx on January 29, 2017.

Clance, P. R., & Imes, S. A. (1978). The imposter phenomenon in high achieving women: Dynamics and therapeutic intervention. *Psychotherapy: Theory, Research and Practice, 15*(3), 241–247.

Clarke, J. H. (2003). *Changing systems to personalize learning: Personalized learning.* Providence, RI: The Education Alliance at Brown University. Accessed at www.brown.edu/academics/education-alliance/sites/brown.edu.academics.education-alliance/files/publications/Personalized_Learning.pdf on October 19, 2017.

Collaboration. (n.d.). In *Merriam-Webster's online dictionary.* Accessed at www.merriam-webster.com/dictionary/collaboration on September 25, 2017.

Collins, J. (2001). *Good to great: Why some companies make the leap . . . and others don't.* New York: Harper Business.

Conzemius, A. E., & O'Neill, J. (2014). *The handbook for SMART school teams: Revitalizing best practices for collaboration* (2nd ed.). Bloomington, IN: Solution Tree Press.

Costa, P. T., & McRae, R. R. (1992). *Revised NEO personality inventory (NEO PI-R) and NEO five-factor inventory (NEO-FFI).* Odessa, FL: Psychological Assessment Resources.

Cramer, K. D. (2014). *Lead positive: What highly effective leaders see, say, and do.* San Francisco: Jossey-Bass.

Deal, T. E., & Peterson, K. D. (1999). *Shaping school culture: The heart of leadership.* San Francisco: Jossey-Bass.

DeAngelis, T. (2003). Why we overestimate our competence: Social psychologists are examining people's pattern of overlooking their own weaknesses. *Monitor on Psychology, 34*(2), 60–62. Accessed at www.apa.org/monitor/feb03/overestimate.aspx on October 27, 2017.

de Vries, R. E., Bakker-Pieper, A., & Oostenveld, W. (2010). Leadership = communication? The relations of leaders' communication styles with leadership styles, knowledge sharing and leadership outcomes. *Journal of Business and Psychology, 25*(3), 367–380. Accessed at https://link.springer.com/article/10.1007/s10869-009-9140-2 on November 5, 2017.

DuFour, R. (2015). *In praise of American educators: And how they can become even better.* Bloomington, IN: Solution Tree Press.

DuFour, R., DuFour, R., Eaker, R., & Karhanek, G. (2004). *Whatever it takes: How professional learning communities respond when kids don't learn.* Bloomington, IN: Solution Tree Press.

DuFour, R., DuFour, R., Eaker, R., & Karhanek, G. (2010). *Raising the bar and closing the gap: Whatever it takes.* Bloomington, IN: Solution Tree Press.

DuFour, R., DuFour, R., Eaker, R., Many, T. W., & Mattos, M. (2016). *Learning by doing: A handbook for Professional Learning Communities at Work* (3rd ed.). Bloomington, IN: Solution Tree Press.

DuFour, R., & Fullan, M. (2013). *Cultures built to last: Systemic PLCs at Work.* Bloomington, IN: Solution Tree Press.

DuFour, R., & Marzano, R. J. (2011). *Leaders of learning: How district, school, and classroom leaders improve student achievement.* Bloomington, IN: Solution Tree Press.

Duhigg, C. (2016, February 25). What Google learned on its quest to build the perfect team. *The New York Times Magazine.* Accessed at www.nytimes.com/2016/02/28/magazine/what-google-learned-from-its-quest-to-build-the-perfect-team.html on November 21, 2017.

Eaker, R., & Keating, J. (2012). *Every school, every team, every classroom: District leadership for growing Professional Learning Communities at Work.* Bloomington, IN: Solution Tree Press.

Edmonds, R. (1979). Effective schools for the urban poor. *Educational Leadership, 37*(1), 15–18. Accessed at https://pdfs.semanticscholar.org/550b/740eb13c411d36d38f498293472cf64fdcef.pdf on February 2, 2018.

Edmonson, A. C. (2004). Psychological safety, trust, and learning in organizations: A group-level lens. In R. M. Kramer & K. S. Cook (Eds.), *Trust and distrust in organizations: Dilemmas and approaches* (pp. 239–272). New York: Russell Sage Foundation.

Erkens, C. (2008). Growing teacher leadership. In *The collaborative administrator: Working together as a professional learning community* (pp. 39–53). Bloomington, IN: Solution Tree Press.

Fullan, M. (1992). *Successful school improvement: The implementation perspective and beyond.* Philadelphia: Open University Press.

Fullan, M. (2001). *Leading in a culture of change.* San Francisco: Jossey-Bass.

Fullan, M. (2007). *The new meaning of educational change* (4th ed.). New York: Teachers College Press.

George, B. (2011, February 26). Leadership skills start with self-awareness. *Minnesota StarTribune.* Accessed at www.startribune.com/leadership-skills-start-with-self-awareness/116923928 on October 23, 2017.

Gilbert, D. T., Giesler, R. B., & Morris, K. A. (1995). When comparisons arise. *Journal of Personality and Social Psychology, 69*(2), 227–236. Accessed at www.ncbi.nlm.nih.gov/pubmed/7643304 on October 17, 2017.

Hackman, J. R. (2002). *Leading teams: Setting the stage for great performances.* Boston: Harvard Business School.

Hattie, J. (2009). *Visible learning: A synthesis of over 800 meta-analyses relating to achievement.* New York: Routledge.

Hunter, J. C. (2004). *The world's most powerful leadership principle: How to become a servant leader*. New York: Crown Business.

Ibarra, H. (2015). *Act like a leader, think like a leader*. Boston: Harvard Business Review Press.

Jarvenpaa, S. L., Knoll, K., & Leidner, D. E. (1998). Is anybody out there? Antecedents of trust in global virtual teams. *Journal of Management Information Systems, 14*(4), 29–64. Accessed at https://pdfs.semanticscholar.org/43c8/f25b626cb154969a61cc26c94936b62a3091.pdf on October 17, 2017.

Kanold, T. D. (2011). *The five disciplines of PLC leaders*. Bloomington, IN: Solution Tree Press.

Kotter, J. P. (2012). *Leading change*. Boston: Harvard Business Review Press.

Kouzes, J. M., & Posner, B. Z. (1999). *Encouraging the heart: A leader's guide to encouraging and recognizing others*. San Francisco: Jossey-Bass.

Kouzes, J. M., & Posner, B. Z. (2011). *Credibility: How leaders gain and lose it, why people demand it*. San Francisco: Jossey-Bass.

Kouzes, J. M., & Posner, B. Z. (2012). *The leadership challenge: How to make extraordinary things happen in organizations* (5th ed.). San Francisco: Jossey-Bass.

Kramer, S. V. (2015). *How to leverage PLCs for school improvement*. Bloomington, IN: Solution Tree Press.

Kruger, J., & Dunning, D. (1999). Unskilled and unaware of it: How difficulties in recognizing one's own incompetence lead to inflated self-assessments. *Journal of Personality and Social Psychology, 77*(6), 1121–1134. Accessed at http://psych.colorado.edu/~vanboven/teaching/p7536_heurbias/p7536_readings/kruger_dunning.pdf on October 27, 2017.

Lambert, L. (1998). *Building leadership capacity in schools*. Alexandria, VA: Association for Supervision and Curriculum Development.

Lens, W., Paixão, M. P., Herrera, D., & Grobler, A. (2012). Future time perspective as a motivational variable: Content and extension of future goals affect the quantity and quality of motivation. *Japanese Psychological Research, 54*(3), 321–333. Abstract accessed at http://onlinelibrary.wiley.com/doi/10.1111/j.1468-5884.2012.00520.x/abstract on November 5, 2017.

Lezotte, L. W. (1991). *Correlates of effective schools: The first and second generation*. Okemos, MI: Effective Schools Products. Accessed at www.effectiveschools.com/images/stories/escorrelates.pdf on April 7, 2017.

Lipton, L., & Wellman, B. (2012). *Got data? Now what? Creating and leading cultures of inquiry.* Bloomington, IN: Solution Tree Press.

Madsen, J. (1996). *Private and public school partnerships: Sharing lessons about decentralization.* London: Falmer Press.

Marzano, R. J. (2003). *What works in schools: Translating research into action.* Alexandria, VA: Association for Supervision and Curriculum Development.

Marzano, R. J. (2017). *The new art and science of teaching.* Bloomington, IN: Solution Tree Press.

Marzano, R. J. (2018). *Making classroom assessments reliable and valid.* Bloomington, IN: Solution Tree Press.

Marzano, R. J., Heflebower, T., Hoegh, J. K., Warrick, P., & Grift, G. (2016). *Collaborative teams that transform schools: The next steps in PLCs.* Bloomington, IN: Marzano Research.

Marzano, R. J., Warrick, P., & Simms, J. A. (2014). *A handbook for high reliability schools: The next step in school reform.* Bloomington, IN: Marzano Research.

Marzano, R. J., & Waters, T. (2009). *District leadership that works: Striking the right balance.* Bloomington, IN: Solution Tree Press.

Marzano, R. J., Waters, T., & McNulty, B. A. (2005). *School leadership that works: From research to results.* Alexandria, VA: Association for Supervision and Curriculum Development.

Mattos, M., DuFour, R., DuFour, R., Eaker, B., & Many, T. W. (2016). *Concise answers to frequently asked questions about Professional Learning Communities at Work.* Bloomington, IN: Solution Tree Press.

Maxwell, J. C. (2016). *What successful people know about leadership: Advice from America's #1 leadership authority.* New York: Center Street.

Muhammad, A. (2018). *Transforming school culture: How to overcome staff division* (2nd ed.). Bloomington, IN: Solution Tree Press.

Muhammad, A., & Hollie, S. (2012). *The will to lead, the skill to teach: Transforming schools at every level.* Bloomington, IN: Solution Tree Press.

Murphy, S. (2002). *Future protocol: a.k.a. back to the future.* Accessed at www.nsrfharmony.org/system/files/protocols/future.pdf on October 19, 2017.

O'Connell, D. J., Hickerson, K., & Pillutla, A. (2011). Organizational visioning: An integrative review. *Group and Organization Management, 36*(1), 103–125. Accessed at www.researchgate.net/publication/253507916_Organizational_Visioning_An_Integrative_Review on November 5, 2017.

O'Neill, J., & Conzemius, A. (2006). *The power of SMART goals: Using goals to improve student learning.* Bloomington, IN: Solution Tree Press.

Pentland, A. (2012, April). The new science of building great teams. *Harvard Business Review.* Accessed at https://hbr.org/2012/04/the-new-science-of-building-great-teams on October 17, 2017.

Peterson, J. (2016). *The 10 laws of trust: Building the bonds that make a business great.* New York: American Management Association.

Rath, T., & Conchie, B. (2008). *Strengths based leadership: Great leaders, teams, and why people follow.* New York: Gallup Press.

Rigoni, B., & Nelson, B. (2016, May 17). The matrix: Teams are gaining greater power in companies. *Gallup Business Journal.* Accessed at http://news.gallup.com/businessjournal/191516/matrix-teams-gaining-greater-power-companies.aspx?g_source=BUILDING_TEAMS&g_medium=topic&g_campaign=tiles on November 1, 2017.

Sebring, P. B., & Bryk, A. S. (2000). School leadership and the bottom line in Chicago. *Phi Delta Kappan, 81*(6), 440–443.

South Dakota Department of Education. (n.d.). *Student enrollment data.* Accessed at http://doe.sd.gov/ofm/enrollment.aspx on January 29, 2018.

Sparks, D. (2005). *Leading for results: Transforming teaching, learning, and relationships in schools.* Thousand Oaks, CA: Corwin Press.

Sparks, D. (2010). *Leadership 180: Daily meditations on school leadership.* Bloomington, IN: Solution Tree Press.

Stark, M. (2002, July 15). *Leading teams: Setting the stage for great performances—The five keys to successful teams.* Boston: Harvard Business School. Accessed at https://hbswk.hbs.edu/archive/leading-teams-setting-the-stage-for-great-performances-the-five-keys-to-successful-teams on November 1, 2017.

Taggar, S., & Ellis, R. (2007). The role of leaders in shaping formal team norms. *The Leadership Quarterly, 18*(2), 105–120. Accessed at www.sciencedirect.com/science/article/pii/S1048984307000033 on November 5, 2017.

Thomas, J., & McDonagh, D. (2013). Shared language: Towards more effective communication. *Australasian Medical Journal, 6*(1), 46–54. Accessed at www.ncbi.nlm.nih.gov/pmc/articles/PMC3575067 on November 5, 2017.

Thoms, P., & Greenberger, D. B. (1998). A test of vision training and potential antecedents to leaders' visioning ability. *Human Resource Development Quarterly, 9*(1), 3–19. Abstract accessed at http://onlinelibrary.wiley.com/doi/10.1002/hrdq.3920090102/full on November 5, 2017.

Tschannen-Moran, M., & Hoy, W. K. (1998). Trust in schools: A conceptual and empirical analysis. *Journal of Educational Administration, 36*(4), 334–352. Accessed at www.researchgate.net/publication/235295498_A_Conceptual_and_Empirical_Analysis_of_Trust_in_Schools on October 19, 2017.

Vodicka, D. (2006). The four elements of trust: Consistency, compassion, communication, and competency. *Principal Leadership, 7*(3), 27–30. Accessed at www.plcwashington.org/cms/lib/WA07001774/Centricity/Domain/38/4-elements-of-trust.pdf on October 30, 2017.

Whitener, E. M., Brodt, S. E., Korsgaard, M. A., & Werner, J. M. (1998). Managers as initiators of trust: An exchange relationship framework for understanding managerial trustworthy behavior. *Academy of Management Review, 23*(3), 513–530. Accessed at http://portal.psychology.uoguelph.ca/faculty/gill/7140/WEEK_5_Feb.6/Whitener%20et%20al._AMR1998.pdf on October 30, 2017.

Zes, D., & Landis, D. (2013). *A better return on self-awareness: Companies with higher rates of return on stock also have employees with few personal blind spots.* Los Angeles, CA: Korn Ferry Institute. Accessed at www.kornferry.com/institute/647-a-better-return-on-self-awareness on October 23, 2017.

INDEX

Amplify Your Impact
Thomas W. Many, Michael J. Maffoni, Susan K. Sparks, and Tesha Ferriby Thomas
Now is the time to improve collaboration in your PLC. Using the latest research on coaching and collaboration, the authors share concrete action steps your school can take to adopt proven collaborative coaching methods, fortify teacher teams, and ultimately improve student learning in classrooms.
BKF794

Building Great School Board–Superintendent Teams
Bradley V. Balch and Michael T. Adamson
Effectively address urgent challenges and drive continuous improvement by developing strong school board–superintendent teams. The authors offer a systematic approach for establishing a team that can efficiently address demands, avoid conflict, and respond to the ever-changing educational environment.
BKF787

Messaging Matters
William D. Parker
Harness the power of messaging to create a culture of acknowledgment, respect, and celebration. Written especially for leaders, this title is divided into three parts, helping readers maximize their role as chief communicators with students, teachers, and parents and community.
BKF785

Transforming School Culture, Second Edition
Anthony Muhammad
The second edition of this best-selling resource delivers powerful new insight into the four types of educators and how to work with each group to create thriving schools. The book also includes Dr. Muhammad's latest research and a new chapter of frequently asked questions.
BKF793

Solution Tree | Press

Visit SolutionTree.com or call 800.733.6786 to order.